"The power of *The Elimination* lies in the telling details Mr. Panh employs to describe the madness of these years, when the Khmer Rouge worked to destroy every vestige of individuality . . . a searing, firsthand account of the Cambodian genocide and as such an important contribution to the history of those years. It is also an examination of the nature of evil as told from the perspectives of a victim and a perpetrator." —*Wall Street Journal*

"In this astounding work, Rithy Panh presents the atrocities of the Khmer Rouge regime as universal human history, intelligible to us all thanks to the extraordinary efforts of an individual."

—Timothy Snyder, best-selling author of *On Tyranny* and *On Freedom*

"Having survived the 'killing fields,' Rithy Panh now illuminates them, both through his own wrenching recollections and his extraordinary interviews with Comrade Duch, a banal mastermind behind the Cambodian genocide. That *The Elimination* is so elegantly understated makes it even more searing—and essential."

—David Margolick, journalist and author of *The Promise and the Dream*

"Like no other book, *The Elimination* reminds us why it is crucial to study history, why education should be a nation's highest priority, and why nothing is more important than culture and the arts. Masterfully written with the language and pacing necessary to tell such a story, *The Elimination* needs to be read by anyone who reads books—and more importantly, by those who don't." —*Coffin Factory*

"Harrowing personal reflections by the Cambodian French filmmaker of surviving the Khmer Rouge as a young teenager . . . A riveting, intimate look deep inside the machinery of the executioner." —*Kirkus*

"In *The Elimination*, a book beautifully written—and obviously in deep friendship—with Christophe Bataille, something is reborn. Perhaps hope."
—Claude Lanzmann, filmmaker and author of
The Patagonian Hare, in *Le Point*

"In the tradition of a Primo Levi or a Solzhenitsyn, the Franco-Cambodian cinéaste Rithy Panh has published an exceptional testimony in which he tells of how he survived the genocide orchestrated by the Khmer Rouge between 1975 and 1979." —*Le Figaro*

"This is a great text, humble in tone and with universal import. We greet it today in the tradition of Jean Hatzfeld. For his part, Rithy Panh takes his place among those rare figures who have shared Vladimir Jankélévitch's conviction: *It's not enough to be sublime, one must be faithful and serious.*" —*Le Monde*

"An exceptional document of Primo Levi's caliber...Rithy Panh's book, *The Elimination*, through its strength, the starkness of its language, and the depths of its mystery, shows its significance." —*Elle* (France)

"With the help of Christophe Bataille, the Cambodian cinéaste Rithy Panh, having survived the Khmer Rouge massacres of the terrible years 1975–1979, gives us an incredibly powerful book. A book? More like a punch in the stomach! . . . It is also a book with caustic intelligence, the slow deconstruction of a mad system . . . this book will remain inscribed in me as major." —*Libération*

"*The Elimination* is a searing, firsthand account of the Cambodian genocide and as such an important contribution to the history of those years. It is also an examination of the nature of evil as told from the perspectives of a victim and a perpetrator." —*Hudson Institute*

"Woven like cross-stitches into this patchwork narrative of a life stripped bare, in which [Panh's] parents, siblings, and relatives wilted under increasingly extreme conditions, is a larger meditation on the forces galvanizing the destruction." —*Asia Times*

THE
ELIMINATION

OTHER PRESS

NEW YORK

THE
ELIMINATION

A SURVIVOR OF THE KHMER ROUGE

CONFRONTS HIS PAST AND THE COMMANDANT

OF THE KILLING FIELDS

RITHY PANH

WITH CHRISTOPHE BATAILLE

TRANSLATED BY JOHN CULLEN

Copyright © Éditions Grasset & Fasquelle, 2012
Originally published in French as *L'élimination* by Éditions Grasset & Fasquelle.

Translation copyright © 2012 John Cullen

Introduction to the 2025 edition translation copyright © 2024 Luke Leafgren

This work, published as part of a program providing publication assistance, received financial support from the French Ministry of Foreign Affairs, the Cultural Services of the French Embassy in the United States, and FACE (French American Cultural Exchange).

Production Editor: Yvonne E. Cárdenas
Book design: Chris Welch
This book was set in 11.5 pt Bembo by Alpha Design & Composition
of Pittsfield, NH.

10 9 8 7 6 5 4 3 2 1

Library of Congress Cataloging-in-Publication Data
Names: Rithy Panh, author. | Bataille, Christophe, author. |
Cullen, John, 1942- translator.
Title: The elimination : a survivor of the Khmer Rouge confronts his past and the commandant of the Killing Fields / Rithy Panh with Christophe Bataille ; translated by John Cullen.
Other titles: Élimination. English | Survivor of the Khmer Rouge confronts his past and the commandant of the Killing Fields
Description: New York : Other Press, [2025] | "Originally published in French as "L'élimination" by Éditions Grasset & Fasquelle." | Includes bibliographical references.
Identifiers: LCCN 2024055411 (print) | LCCN 2024055412 (ebook) | ISBN 9781635425581 (paperback) | ISBN 9781635425727 (ebook)
Subjects: LCSH: Rithy Panh. | Kang, Kech Ieu, 1942- | Parti communiste du Kampuchea. | Genocide survivors—Cambodia—Biography. | Political refugees—Cambodia—Biography. | Political atrocities—Cambodia. | Cambodia—Politics and government--1975-1979. | Phnom Penh (Cambodia)—Biography.
Classification: LCC DS554.83.R58 A313 2025 (print) | LCC DS554.83.R58 (ebook) | DDC 959.604/2092 [B]—dc23/eng/20241231
LC record available at https://lccn.loc.gov/2024055411
LC ebook record available at https://lccn.loc.gov/2024055412

To my father, Panh Lauv

To Vann Nath

Duch: "Mr. Rithy,
you've forgotten an even more important
slogan: 'The blood debt must be repaid by blood.'"

I'm surprised: "Why that slogan?
Why not one that's more ideological?"

Duch fixes me with his eyes:
"The Khmer Rouge were all about elimination.
Human rights didn't exist."

INTRODUCTION TO THE 2025 EDITION

TRANSLATED BY LUKE LEAFGREN

FIFTY YEARS AGO, the capital of Cambodia fell to the Khmer Rouge. From April 1975 through January 1979, my country experienced a radical transformation and a radical suffering—called here by one of its great torturers, in a word of absolute truth, "the elimination."

I have tried to approach this revolution. To approach it like the boy I was, whose life and whose entire family had been carried off from the very first day by hunger, fear, sickness, and death—all of it fully desired and organized by the revolutionary regime. That boy of fourteen years, now become a man, devotes part of his cinematic work to documenting the crimes of the Khmer Rouge: filming the places—possibly a well, a pond, an execution field—often invisible or impossible to comprehend; filming the beings, survivors, witnesses, historians, deniers, executioners. But also the documents and the objects, particularly in Security

Prison 21: torture files, drawings, chains, graffiti, dug-up soil, portraits of Pol Pot.

With the passage of time and age, I decided to film Duch, the commandant of S-21, dedicated ideologue and quintessential trainer in the Khmer Rouge death machine. Four hundred hours face-to-face in the prison of Phnom Penh, from which I distilled the documentary *Duch, Master of the Forges of Hell.*

Our pact of truth was clear: every question was possible—every answer too, I feared. But the use of images, and how they were edited and analyzed, was up to me. Of course, this work of cinema and writing is not preventing mass death, but it clarifies a certain appeal of death at the heart of the revolutionary ideal. Am I a monster? Am I not a monster? That's the kind of question that Duch seems not to ask himself. And his education, his ideology, his assertive and spirited fortitude, even his romantic history seem to answer in the negative: they show the man, his original dream, his fight. And they say to us, the spectators, in a severe and ironic tone: You, Mr. Rithy, would have been an excellent commandant of S-21, just like me.

But if there is an enigma, possibly about the monstrous being, there is no mystery about the vocation of evil.

To approach this man, and to come back to him again today, is a painful discipline, but I try to follow it as my rule. To speak to the man. To speak at human height, with the physical possibility of seeing his eyes, his mouth, his hands, and even to touch him. To repeat, and to accept the repetition as part of the process of truth. To let time unfold in the world of speaking, of forgetting, of lying, of doubt, of silence. And finally, to refrain from big words, if they exist, which are always a screen, a protection, the first step toward violence.

As you will read in these pages, to form an opinion about a historical event like this does not for me entail moderation, which would be a confession, nor neutrality, which is ontologically impossible, but rather it entails going physically upon the land—to commit one's body, one's skin, one's eyes, one's sweat, one's emotions. And believe me, when you scratch rice paddies under the sun with your fingernails, only to find bones, then you can begin to speak about the crime. It is also this leap that I propose to you.

DUCH DIED IN his own secure prison, yet evil persists, everywhere. I believe that he was not a monster, and I still regret that he was not set free after his conviction in 2010. The adversary left me neither joy nor grief. I learned that he had, near the end, formally renounced Christianity. I know nothing more, but it's an intriguing symbol, perhaps a trick of historical reason, for a fanatic Marxist-Leninist militant ultimately to renounce this private, spiritual revolution. I hope he felt a sense of being abandoned by God, and also what forgiveness must be: not granted to himself,

with one hand on a Bible, but requested and unmerited—
and without a doubt, never fully obtained. What this man
committed was not a sin, but an extraction from the world
of humanity, which nothing can redeem, neither in this
world nor in any other. But renouncing his late conversion to Christianity is perhaps the return to a protective
pride—so clearly did salvation appear to be within reach,
and almost legitimately exchanged. Yet Duch never publicly named what he did—starting with the M-13 detention
and execution center, deep in the jungle, when he was a
young man and already familiar with the ideology and the
life of a guerrilla. M-13 was the first transposition of pure
revolutionary ideas into action: hunting down "enemies of
the state," torture, paranoia. Duch never publicly named
what he inflicted upon the young Bophana, horribly tortured for weeks at S-21, under his violent, masculine rule.
Bophana, whose only crime was to love her husband, Hout
Ly, and whose torture file was the thickest in all the camp.
Even today, it is easier, or more tempting, to see in Duch an
abstract version of the French revolutionary Louis Antoine
de Saint-Just, rather than an evil man ready for beatings, for
rape, ready to destroy a being—with nothing more than a
mark in his notebooks in pretty mauve ink.

GOING BACK TO the village: the ability, peaceful or cruel, of
this old man to be alone, to dress himself, to feed himself,

to wash himself, to look at the sky, at neighbors, and to see them observing him in this world; the ability to find himself confronted with his childhood, his places, his images, his nights, his sophisticated methods of death, his ordinary crimes—far from big words. Alone, comrade. Alone. The Khmer Rouge revolution is over.

FIFTY YEARS AFTER the fall of Phnom Penh, I am still searching, we are still searching, for images, records, songs, writings, signs—all destined to become our historical archives, and not just the archives of the crime. It's true that in their obsession with destructive purity, the Khmer Rouge wanted to erase the individual human being and the social classes, erase to the point of obliteration. This began through an immediate upheaval in language, with the appearance of certain words, the reversal and often the perversion of other terms, and above all by the spread of slogans. Always political, often easy to remember, and sometimes poetic in their naively agrarian character, though in reality cynical and cruel. Repeated a thousand and one times, as I experienced over four years, they simultaneously empty and fill.

This archival work is always fascinating, and it shows a clear gap with regard to the evil employed today on so many continents. The digital revolution permits live documentation of the crime. Even more, it allows it to be claimed and affirmed, to be staged internationally and emotionally. It's a historical compilation without precedent: to offer the world appalling images of rape, torture, beheadings, executions, kidnappings, desperate faces; to confirm that the creator and disseminator of those images will certainly be identified, and that he shares out his passion for evil like a mad frenzy, like an inhuman revel. And this hideous carousing, which can be difficult to tear yourself away from, is accompanied by a radical ideological position. No glorious transformation, nor a strategic pursuit of liberty, but the passion for death. Against this spectacle that lashes us, filmed from a motorbike in the desert or the jungle, in public squares, I can offer only the meager weapons of my work.

I spare myself mindless comparisons, big words, proud positions. Is this a method? A wisdom born of experience? In any case, it's not quietism. Like Stefan Zweig, I believe there exists a "resistance of the truth," even if it cannot be uttered or achieved in a day. Evil is complex, unique, sometimes exciting, often masked. Sometimes it is found in a blinding light, sometimes on continents entirely invisible. I myself know great minds, celebrated for their accomplishments, who discern crime or genocide with force and speed, or the theory of a revolution, but who are unable to revisit their past writings. Would they read grave historical errors there? Could they make an intellectual analysis of their blind progression?

But the fight for the good, for knowledge, for beauty—yes, let's not forget this weapon, never ridiculous—continues.

IN APRIL 1975, I was fourteen years old. Each year, I think of my poor birthday, upon the roads of Cambodia, and of my mother, exhausted and anxious, selling her beautiful sheets to offer us, my father and us children, a celebratory meal of several pork ribs rolled in the coals. I fight sadness by continuing to live with my missing family members. A great pessimism comes over me. So all beauty surprises me. Some time ago, I discovered the plateaus of the Upper Loire, forested and wild. I walk there in summer, on paths surrounded by trees and ferns, and by sounds and smells I'm unable to recognize. I run with the wind in my face, and it cleanses thoughts, images, and sometimes it reminds me of other cool nights of a childhood forever lost. I swim in the gorges, I follow the river, the grass tenderly brushes me, and how empty the sky is here! So, I am alive.

The world is never far, and I do not flee it. I try not to be, as Walter Benjamin wrote about revolution, the tiger that leaps into the past. On this land, I find a little peace. The living. Standing together. Actions. Simple. There is no paradise outside this world, only a landscape from which nothing can tear me away. I love this bread, raised in the oven. The postman and the meal he brings to the elderly. These nearly deserted kilometers—without news of the world, without crises written in capital letters, without angry crowds or spiteful billionaires. I love these views, snow-covered nature in January, with its black heights and icy wind, but also the horses, the cows, the long-suffering donkey frozen in place. I observe stone walls, the color of volcanoes. And all the woods, chopped, smooth, split, gloriously raised, poor and sculpted. I think of Monet, who described "catching [himself], eyes fixed on the tragic temple, seeking what comes next, the degradations of color that death had just imposed on the motionless face"—that of his beloved wife, dead. But the artistic work continues.

When visiting the nearby castle, I feel like a petty lord. It was built in the eleventh century, and little remains, arches, beams, vague piles, images of combat and lookouts. From a distance, the waiting, the adversary, the ideal. That was also the century of Angkor, the glory of the kingdom subsequently abandoned. Now I hold these two grandeurs in my pagan gaze. I was not fully eliminated by the Khmer Rouge. Enter with me into this world for a few hours; think of my brothers and sisters, my parents, the terrible fields of Cambodia; think of the spirit of revolution, and of each of our words. And don't forget to breathe.

THE
ELIMINATION

KAING GUEK EAV, known as Comrade Duch, was the commandant of Security Prison 21—the S-21 torture and execution center in Phnom Penh, Cambodia—from 1975 to 1979. He chose his nom de guerre, he explains, from a book he remembers reading in his childhood; in the book little Duch was a "good boy."

At least 12,380 people were tortured in that prison. After the victims confessed, they were executed in the "killing field" of Choeung Ek (also under Duch's command), about ten miles southeast of Phnom Penh. In S-21 no one escaped torture. No one escaped death.

We're inside the walls of another prison, the one to which Duch was sentenced in 2010 by the ECCC, the Extraordinary Chambers in the Courts of Cambodia, a national court (better known as the Khmer Rouge Tribunal) backed by the United Nations.

He speaks to me in his soft voice, "S-21 was the end of the line. People who got sent there were already corpses. Human or animal? That's another subject."

I observe his face, the face of an old man, his large, almost dreamy eyes, his ruined left hand. I envision his younger features and discern the cruelty and madness of his thirties. I understand that he may have had the ability to fascinate, but I'm not afraid. I'm at peace.

SOME YEARS PREVIOUSLY, in preparation for my film *S21: The Khmer Rouge Killing Machine*, I conducted long interviews with guards, torturers, executioners, photographers, nurses, and drivers who had served under Duch's command. Very few of them have had to face legal proceedings. All of them are now free. Sitting in a former cell in S-21—the torture center has been turned into a museum—one of them blurts out, "The prisoners? They were like pieces of wood." He laughs nervously.

At the same table, before a picture of Pol Pot, another one explains, "Prisoners have no rights. They're half human and half corpse. They're not humans, and they're not corpses. They're soulless, like animals. You're not afraid to hurt them. We weren't worried about our karma."

I ask Duch, too, if he has nightmares: from having authorized electrocutions, beatings with cords, the thrusting of needles under fingernails; from having made people eat excrement; from having recorded confessions that were lies; from having given orders to slit the throats of men and women lined up blindfolded at the edge of a ditch and deafened by a roaring generator. He considers for a while and then answers me with lowered eyes: "No." Later, I film him laughing.

I DON'T LIKE the overused word "trauma." Today, every individual, every family has its trauma, whether large or small. In my case, it manifests itself as unending desolation; as ineradicable images, gestures no longer possible, silences that pursue me. I ask Duch if he used to dream at night in his cell in the tribunal's prison. A man who has commanded a place like S-21, and before that M-13, another detention and execution center in the jungle—doesn't such a man see in nightmares the agonized faces of his victims, calling to him and asking him why? The face, perhaps, of the young and beautiful Bophana, twenty years old, who was savagely tortured for several months?

As for me, ever since the Khmer Rouge were driven from power in 1979, I've never stopped thinking about my family. I see my sisters, my big brother and his guitar, my brother-in-law, my parents. All dead. Their faces are talismans. I see my little nephew and niece again—how old are they? five and seven?—starving, breathing with difficulty, staring into space, panting. I remember their last days, their knowing bodies. I remember helplessness. Childish lips closed tight. Duch seems surprised by my question. He thinks for a bit and then says simply, "Dream? No. Never."

IF I CLOSE my eyes, still today, everything comes back to me. The dried-up rice fields. The road that runs through the village, not far from Battambang. Men dressed in black, outlined against the burning horizon. I'm thirteen years old. I'm alone. If I keep my eyes shut, I see the path. I know where the mass grave is, behind Mong hospital; all I have to do is stretch out my hand, and the ditch will be in front of me. But I open my eyes in time. I won't see that new morning or the freshly dug earth or the yellow cloth we wrapped the bodies in. I've seen enough faces. They're rigid, grimacing. I've buried enough men with swollen bellies and open mouths. People say their souls will wander all over the earth.

Now I'm a man in my turn. I'm far away. I'm alive. I no longer remember names or dates: the village boss who used to go horseback riding in the country; the woman who was forced into marriage; the worksites where I slept; the loudspeakers blaring in the morning. I no longer know them. What wounds me has no name.

I'm not looking for objective truth today; I just want words. Especially Duch's words. I want him to talk and explain himself. To tell his truth, to describe his path, to say what he was, what he wanted or believed himself to be. He has, after all, lived a life; he's living it now; he's been a man and even a child. I want this son of an incompetent, debt-ridden businessman, this brilliant student, this mathematics professor so respected by his own students, this revolutionary who still quotes Balzac and Alfred de

Vigny, this dialectician, this chief executioner, this master of torture—I want him to answer me, and in so doing to take a step on the road to humanity.

IN 1979 I LAND in Grenoble, where I'm welcomed by my family. I tell them little or nothing about what I've been through. In a short piece written in Khmer, I recount those four years, 1975 to 1979. With the passage of time those old pages will vanish. I'll never see them again. And talking is difficult.

I start school and begin to discover the country I've dreamed about so much, and freedom. The weather's cold and dark. I can't read or write or speak French, or so little as makes no difference. I'm elsewhere. I have few friends. What can I say, and to whom? Very quickly I turn to painting. I copy. I sketch. I draw barbed wire and skulls. Men in striped clothes. Metal arches guarded by dogs. Then I take up the guitar and discover woodworking.

One day a huge schoolmate corners me in the corridor and strikes me on the head. This makes his pals laugh. He hits me once, twice, three times. I plead with him to stop because in Cambodia the head is sacred. But he keeps it up. My back's to the wall, and suddenly everything turns upside down. Incredible strength comes into my hands, I fling myself on him, I strike out in turn. A veil falls. An instant later I open my eyes: the guy's lying on the ground, curled up, with blood all over his face. I'm being held back; other arms pin my arms. I'm breathing hard. I'm trembling.

In the following months, fearing reprisals, I carried a metal pipe wrapped in newspaper in my schoolbag. Fortunately I never had to use the thing.

And so violence abides. The evil done to me is inside me. Present and powerful. Lying in wait. Many years, many encounters, many tears, and much reading will be necessary for me to overcome it. I don't like the thought of that bloody morning, and thirty years later I don't like recounting it either. I'm not ashamed; I'm just reluctant.

Drawing and woodworking were pushing me into silence. I chose film, which shows the world, presents beauty, and also deals in words. I figure it keeps my fists in my pockets.

Ever since that episode I'm wary of violence. I stay away from weapons. And I avoid stairwells, terraces, precipices, unobstructed views, cliffs. Falling is easy. And I've already lived so much. If I'm on a balcony, I can't help myself— I calculate how many seconds I'd fall before hitting the ground. But I don't give in. And I'm going to meet Duch with my camera and film hundreds of hours of interviews. I need to have him in front of me. Maybe my movie project is nothing but an excuse to get close to him. I want those who perpetrated that evil to call it by its name. I want them to talk.

I'D NEVER INTENDED to make a film about Duch, but I didn't like his absence from *S21: The Khmer Rouge Killing Machine*, which is almost entirely an indictment of the man; everybody accuses him. It was as though my investigation was missing an essential element: Duch's words.

I review the images that were never included in *S21*, which required three years to shoot. I wanted to cover the story thoroughly, but also to find the proper distance; not to treat the material as sacred, but not to trivialize it either. First I went to see the torturers in their homes. I spoke to them. I tried to persuade them. Then I filmed them in the very places where their acts had been committed. I often paid someone to take their place in the fields because a shoot could require several days. I gave them room and board. Sometimes they came alone. Sometimes they were accompanied by other "comrade interrogators." They would talk among themselves, take one another's measure. Avoid one another. I wanted to make them draw near and feel the truth, to puncture the small lies and refute the big ones. Then they met the painter Vann Nath, one of the few survivors of the center, a calm and just man.

I film their silences, their faces, their gestures. That's my method. I don't fabricate the event. I create situations in which former Khmer Rouge can think about what they did. And in which the survivors can tell what they suffered.

I ask the executioners the same questions. Ten times, twenty if necessary. Some details appear. Some contradictions.

Some new truths. Their eyes hesitate or evade. One of them remembers having tortured someone at one o'clock in the morning. We meet at that hour in S-21. Artificial light. Whispers. A motorcycle passes. All around us cane toads, rustling sounds in the night, a family of owls.

When I show a torturer from the group known as the "Biters" the photograph of a young girl, his first response is to say he recognizes her. "She confessed. But I never touched her." An hour later he murmurs, "I took up a guava branch. I lashed her with it twice. She pissed on herself. She rolled on the ground, crying. Then she asked for a pen. Since her writing was too bad, I took the pen and wrote out her confession myself." She's accused—she accuses herself—of sabotage: supposedly she injected water into the patients' drips and contaminated the operating room. Is that really credible? I look at the man's downcast eyes, listen to the weak drone of his voice. I only partly believe him. He was very violent with that woman: after three days her clothes were torn and her face exhausted. She stayed in S-21 for a month.

The same man explains that he would torture all through the night and sometimes fall asleep with his prisoner. Can you imagine the soiled shackles at the feet of the wooden chairs? The metal mesh springs where the victim writhed in convulsions before he or she finally slept? The pincers, the iron bars, the needles, the vises? The smell of blood? Every twenty minutes Duch or his deputy Mam Nay would telephone to check on the torturer's progress, and he'd report on how he was doing. Then the torture would resume.

The torturer further explains that over the course of several weeks he obtained almost thirty successive "confessions" from a single prisoner. There must be three copies of every confession; each was about twenty pages long. The most important confession would be typed. Administrative lunacy. Duch would read each confession carefully and return the annotated, underlined text to the torturer with requests for clarification and several new queries. The sessions would resume.

IN MY OFFICE in Phnom Penh there's a wall of metal closets. They contain letters, notebooks, sound recordings, archives, distressing statistics, maps. Next door, in a climate-controlled space, I keep various hard disks with photographs, recorded radio broadcasts, Khmer Rouge propaganda films, statements made by witnesses before the tribunal. The entire Cambodian tragedy is here. The Khmer Rouge took the capital city on April 17, 1975. By the time Vietnamese troops drove them from power in January 1979, the tally was 1.7 million dead, or nearly a third of the population of the country.

As in former times a single, long fan blade is paddling the suffocating air. The city comes to me, with its cries, its horns, its children's laughter, its activity. I open a thick file. I look at the vanished faces. Some of them are dear to me. I know their stories and I've read their confessions. Others come and go in my dreams, but I still don't know their names. What do the dead ask? That we think about them? That we liberate them by bringing the guilty to judgment? Or do they want us to understand *what took place*?

I'm holding a slightly streaked, slightly out-of-focus photograph. It shows Duch entering a banquet hall and apparently smiling at ten or so persons, seated around a table, who aren't looking at him. Like all of us at the time he's wearing a pair of black pants. But he's chosen a dark gray shirt, as he's careful to point out to me. What a mystery: how did that calm young man become one of the cruelest torturers and mass murderers of the twentieth century? He looks as though he broke into the banqueting place. But he's cool and casual. I imagine him in 1943, when he's one year old. His parents go off to work in the fields. His mother's an ethnic Cambodian, his father Chinese. He and his sisters grow up in the province of Kampong Thom. A brilliant pupil, he's singled out and continues his education in the town of Siem Reap before being sent to the prestigious Lycée Sisowath in the capital. In his graduation year he receives the second highest examination scores in the country. He elects to pursue a career as a mathematics teacher and along the way meets Son Sen, a man with a lifelong engagement in revolution and ideology. Son Sen will later be Duch's superior in the Khmer

Rouge hierarchy and a member of the Central Committee of the Communist Party of Cambodia.

Duch is assigned to a lycée in a small town in Kampong Cham, not far from Pol Pot's native province. He's the deputy director of the school when he's convicted of having led a riot and serves three years in prison. When he's released in 1970, he goes underground in the countryside. A year later, he's appointed head of "security services" in the jungle, in what's known as the Special Zone. Until 1975 he's the commandant of the M-13 prison, where it's certain that thousands of Cambodians were tortured and subsequently executed. In M-13 Duch fine-tunes his organization and develops his method: "In 1973, when I was the head of M-13, I recruited children. I chose them according to their class—middle-class peasants and the poor. I put them to work, and later I brought them with me to S-21. Those children were formed by the movement and by hard work. I made them into guards and interrogators. The youngest of them looked after the rabbits. They learned how to guard and interrogate before they learned their alphabet. Their level of culture was very low, but they were loyal to me. I trusted them."

At first Duch makes his rounds on a bicycle; later he uses a Honda motorcycle. Some peasants from Amleang tell me, "When we heard the sound of his bicycle chain, we hid ourselves."

In the foreground of the photograph a woman seems to be suckling an infant. I can see only her straight back, the nape of her neck, her short hair. Duch is categorical: the photo was taken at the banquet given to celebrate the marriage of Comrade Nourn Huy, known as Huy Sre, the head of S-24—an annex of S-21. Later this same comrade would be executed, along with his wife, on Duch's orders. I replace the photograph. Every biography, even if examined in detail, remains an enigma.

AT THE END of the 1990s, during the filming of *S21: The Khmer Rouge Killing Machine*, we could feel the presence of the Khmer Rouge, watching us. Who can believe for a moment that they're no longer in the country? One day, while we were shooting an interview with an escapee from Kraing Ta Chan prison, several men arrived carrying machetes and axes. Very angry men. What to do? Resist. I held on to my camera and shouted, "I know who you are and where you worked. I know every one of you. You, you were a torturer in this prison. Don't deny it. You there, you were a guard. And you were a messenger. You think I arrived here just like that, without preparing myself? You think I don't know you?" They hesitated. Vann Nath and my film crew stood beside me. The men put down their machetes and talked with us. By the end of that trying day I was able to film the torturer, alone.

My documentaries *Bophana* and *S21* were shown in Cambodia. Like me, the country was able to retrace its memory. I felt that those films had brought an episode in my life to a close.

Then Duch's trial began. It seemed far away from me. I believed I was at peace. I'd cautioned the tribunal judges, both Cambodian and international, in advance: The images will tell the story, I said; they'll tell the world what the guilty parties did; they'll show their arrogance, their rigidity, their lies, their methods, their cunning. Think about the Nuremberg Trials! Remember the leading Nazi who stands up and replies "*Nein*" before sitting down again; a sequence like that is worth all analyses. Images are educational and universal.

I read the transcripts of the first hearing in Duch's trial, and they tormented me. I realized I couldn't maintain my distance.

I didn't try to understand Duch, nor did I care to judge him; I wanted to give him a chance to explain, in detail, the death process of which he was the organizer-in-chief. So I asked the judges for permission to conduct interviews with him. I met the man in the visiting room and outlined the two basic principles of my project: he wouldn't be the only person to appear in my film—other witnesses, possibly contradictory, would be used—and every subject would be discussed frankly. Summing up, I said, "I'll be forthright and frank with you. Be forthright and frank with me."

He answered me with a sort of sententious tranquility: "Mr. Rithy, both of us are working for the truth."

FIRST DAY OF SHOOTING. Duch leaves his cell in an armored vehicle, escorted by about fifteen guards. He meets me in one of the tribunal's chambers.

> ME: "What should I call you? Kaing Guek Eav?"
>
> DUCH: "No. Call me Duch."
>
> ME: "Duch? Your S-21 name? You don't want to go back to what you were before?"
>
> DUCH: "No. Why do you want me to hide? I'm Duch. Everybody knows me by that name, and that's what they call me. Call me Duch."

I reeled when he said that.

HE'D SEEN MY DOCUMENTARIES and therefore knew all about my work. He didn't like *S21*, because in that film, he's the subject of some very precise accusations. But in speaking to me about *Bophana*, which tells the story of a young woman who was tortured because she wrote to her lover in romantic, coded language, Duch said, "If you run into Bophana's uncle, please ask him to forgive me. I feel sorry for that man—I did him harm. I'm the one responsible. And if you see her husband's mother, tell her that Duch acknowledges the wrong he did." Then he added, "I don't acknowledge everything that's said in your film, but as commandant of S-21 I take full responsibility." Duch wants to believe that redemption can be bought with words. He disputes the historical truth, and then he declares that he takes full responsibility. In other words I deny what you affirm, but I'll bear the burden of your truth.

I answered him, "Mr. Duch, you take on too much. That's not what we're asking for. To each his own responsibility; the torturers, for example, have accepted theirs. And they're re-counting what happened. What I want is to understand what went on at S-21 during those years. I want you to explain everything to us: your role, the jargon you used, the organization of the prison, the confession process, the executions."

After some ten hours of interviews an excited Duch confided in me, "I had a revelation this morning during my prayers. I was overwhelmed. And then I understood: I must talk to you."

I replied, "That's all I ask." And we continued.

LATER HE LAUGHED and asked me, "What's the hourly rate?" I didn't understand, or rather, I pretended not to understand, because I knew that someone before me had paid a large sum in dollars for an interview. To visit the high executioner himself, the monster, the man . . . what excitement. He repeated his question, pronouncing the words distinctly, "Mr. Rithy, what's the hourly rate?"

I answered, "I can't pay you. And I don't want to. My work is to make the film. You know my conditions. I film you, and I alone am in charge of the editing. You can take it or leave it."

He didn't insist. "I was joking," he said. "You know, journalists are paying one of the photographers from S-21 as much as two hundred dollars for an interview! And he talks a lot of idiotic nonsense!" Duch burst out laughing.

During the course of some months, I questioned him without fear and without hate. In the beginning he would launch into long expositions of Marx's writings, historical materialism, and dialectical materialism. Then he discoursed upon his career, his method, the Khmer Rouge doctrine. He sidestepped. Contradicted himself. Looking at photographs, he seemed at first to recognize neither his victims nor his comrade torturers. Not even Tuy, notorious for his cruelty, whom Duch trained in M-13 and later brought with him to S-21, Tuy the specialist in "difficult cases." Little by little, Duch found his voice again, but the only words he had left were lies.

ON THE DAY when I bring him Bophana's file—the thickest interrogation file to come out of S-21—he finds himself in difficulties. His handwriting is everywhere in the file. You can still perceive, after thirty years, the combativeness, the hatred, the perversity, an excitement that resembles desire.

When I'm requesting more precision, more details, his soft voice interrupts me: "Mr. Rithy, I'm grateful to you for having brought me such a complete file. Thank you very much." Then he rises to go.

Only once do we have a really fierce quarrel. I can feel the tribunal guards behind me, leaning over my shoulders, ready to hold me back. Mechanically lining up his files on the desk so that not a single page is sticking out, Duch keeps repeating, "that's true, that's true" with a faraway look in his wide-open eyes.

Suddenly he stops and stares at me: "Mr. Rithy, we have a problem, the two of us—we don't understand each other." The quarrel proceeds.

I say, speaking forcefully, "What's the use of my coming to meet with you if you lie to me?"

Duch smiles.

"That's true, that's true . . ." he says.

A little later, as he's getting up to go, he laughs and says, "Mr. Rithy, let's not argue anymore. See you tomorrow."

After hundreds of hours of filming, the truth became cruelly apparent to me: I had become that man's instrument. His adviser in some way. His coach. As I've written, I was searching not for truth but for knowledge, for consciousness. Let the words come, I thought. But Duch's words always amounted to the same thing, a game of falsehood. A cruel game. Resulting in a vague saga. With my questions, I'd helped to prepare him for his trial. So: I had survived the Khmer Rouge, I was investigating the human enigma as humanly personified by Duch, and he was using me? I found this idea intolerable.

THE WORLD WAS WOBBLING. I nearly suffocated in the plane. I fell several times while walking in the street. In Paris, I avoided the subways and buses. I'd stare at the crowds of people and tremble. Where were they all going? And where had they come from? The slightest noise would make me jump. I held on to metal, to tiling, to wood, to my relatives, to my books, to paper; I held on to the night.

Then a fog of sounds invaded my brain from morning till evening. I'd hear squealing tires. Radio frequencies. Clashing metal. Weird echoes. I remember spending entire nights walking up and down the big boulevard that passes in front of the Royal Palace in Phnom Penh. I was attuned to the rhythm of the traffic. The blood pounded in my temples. I didn't want to hear anymore. I said to my assistant, "If I don't show up back here tonight, come look for me in front of the palace. Don't leave me on the riverbank. Please. Come for me."

I'd sit on the sidewalk with my head in my hands. No sobs, no thoughts. Around four o'clock in the morning I'd ride through the capital of bad dreams in a motorcycle taxi, with a lump in my throat and the warm wind on my forehead. Small cement buildings. Illuminated pagoda.

Vendors' stalls in the shadows. Twenty years now since the Khmer Rouge fled these broad avenues; but I feel Duch's hand, reaching for my shoulders and the back of my neck. He gropes. I resist. I turn around, shivering.

On my way I see a child sleeping in a vegetable cart. The sky is pale. We're saved.

DUCH REMEMBERS NAMES, places, dates, faces, trajectories with great precision. He's a man of memory. Nothing escapes him. He loves method and doctrine. He never stopped refining the slaughter machine—or its language.

Throughout the filming Duch gauges me. I gauge myself too. I can find but little humanity in what he is. Having been saved by a Buddhist monk as a child he's very familiar with Buddhism, but he's no pawn of fate. He's in control of his life from start to finish, all the way to his late conversion to Christianity—he's presently an evangelical Christian. If it's not one ideology, it's another.

On the wholly human scale: I find in myself nothing but sensations. Everything registers as smells, as images, as sounds. I'm alive, but I'm afraid of not being alive anymore. Of not breathing anymore. The bloodbath has drowned part of me.

I BELIEVE THE INSOMNIA started in 1997 when my film *Rice People* was selected to participate in the main competition at the Cannes International Film Festival. My condition has worsened ever since. I made a little money, and a cruel thought stuck fast in my brain: *I can't share this good fortune with my parents.* Then, all at once, my childhood surfaced again. I shook. I couldn't breathe. That money had to be gone through; it absolutely had to be given away. Let it slip from my hands. Let it vanish and take me with it.

After dark I'd walk down the *Grands Boulevards*, surrounded by prostitutes, petty crooks, tourists, and Parisians adrift in the night. I played various table games—poker, baccarat, chemin de fer—in all the Clichy and République and Bastille casinos and gambling halls. I won fortunes. I remember walking through the streets of Paris with a fortune in my pocket. I lived for those miraculous fifteen minutes—and for this lie: I was rich; I had the world on a string. Then I'd become poor again, thank God. Gamblers lose. I laughed and drank a lot with Arabs, Jews, Armenians, Chinese. We were on the skids. We all knew we were going to lose. Besides that was why we were there. The important thing was to flame out so brightly that nothing was left: no chips, no banknotes, no seven-faced dice, no joyful roulette wheels, no casinos, no gamblers. Nothing. No one.

That life disgusted me. I was foundering in anxiety. I dreamed of Mitterand, suffocating in his coffin. I dreamed I'd been shut up in an oven, beating on the walls and shouting in vain. After some weeks I abandoned the night. Like a good boy I returned to my screenplays, to my films, but sleep wouldn't come back.

ME: "The leaders knew the confessions were false?"

DUCH: "I know! I know. It bothered me! I wanted to compare them with the truth, starting as far back as M-13. But what could I do?"

ME: "So everyone knew the confessions were false?"

DUCH: "Yes, but no one dared to say so! Mr. Rithy, I loved police work, but as a way to get to the truth! I didn't like working the Khmer Rouge way."

SO I RESISTED. I held on. That's why I find the end of Primo Levi's life saddening and irritating. Yes, irritating—the word may surprise, but it's true. The idea that Levi survived deportation to a concentration camp, that he wrote at least one great book, *If This Is a Man*, not to mention *The Truce* and *The Periodic Table,* and that he threw himself down a stairwell fifty years later. . . . It's as if his tormentors finally succeeded, in spite of love, in spite of his books. Their hands reached across time to complete the work of destruction, which never ends. Primo Levi's end terrifies me.

IN THE INTERVIEWS we often bring up the works of Karl Marx, which Duch knows and admires.

> ME: "Mr. Duch, who are the closest followers of Marxism?"
> DUCH: "The illiterate."

People who can't read are the "closest" followers of Marxism. They're the ones who are in arms. And, I may add, they're the ones who obey.

Those who read have access to words, to history, and to the history of words. They know that language shapes, flatters, conceals, enthralls. He who reads reads language itself; he perceives its duplicity, its cruelty, its betrayal. He knows that a slogan is just a slogan. And he's seen others.

IN 1975, I was thirteen years old and happy. My father had been the chief undersecretary to several ministers of education in succession; now he was retired, and a member of the senate. My mother cared for their nine children. My parents, both of them descended from peasant families, believed in knowledge. More than that: they had a taste for it. We lived in a house in a suburb close to Phnom Penh. Ours was a life of ease, with books, newspapers, a radio, and eventually a black-and-white television. I didn't know it at the time, but we were destined to be designated—after the Khmer Rouge entered the capital on April 17 of that year—as "new people," which meant members of the bourgeoisie, intellectuals, landowners. That is, oppressors who were to be reeducated in the countryside—or exterminated.

Overnight I become "new people," or (according to an even more horrible expression) an "April 17." Millions of us are so designated. That date becomes my registration number, the date of my birth into the proletarian revolution. The history of my childhood is abolished. Forbidden. From that day on, I, Rithy Panh, thirteen years old, have no more history, no more family, no more emotions, no more thoughts, no more unconscious. Was there a name? Was there an individual? There's nothing anymore.

What a brilliant idea, to give a hated class a name full of hope: *new people*. This huge group will be transformed by the revolution. Transmuted. Or wiped out forever. As for the "old people" or "ordinary people" they're no longer backward and downtrodden, they become the model to follow—men and women working the lands their ancestors worked or bending over machine tools, revolutionaries rooted in practical life. The "old people" are the heirs of the great Khmer Empire. They are ageless. They built Angkor. They threw its stone images into the jungle and into the water. The women stoop in the rice fields. The men build and repair dikes. They fulfill themselves in and by what they do. They're charged with reeducating us and they have absolute power over us.

The flag of Democratic Kampuchea (the country's new name) bears not a hammer and sickle but an image of the great temple of Angkor. "For more than two thousand years, the Khmer people have lived in utter destitution and the most complete discouragement. . . . If our people were capable of building Angkor Wat, then they are capable of doing anything." (Pol Pot, in a speech broadcast on the radio.)

How many people died on the building sites of the twelfth century? Nobody knows. But what they built expressed a spiritual power and elevation utterly absent from the creations of the Khmer Rouge.

A FEW DAYS before April 17, 1975, one of my father's friends came to our house to warn him, "The Khmer Rouge are getting closer. You and your wife and children should leave. There's still time. We'll find a solution for you—a plane to Thailand, for example. You must flee." My imperturbable father refused to budge. He wasn't afraid. A man devoted to education, he was a servant of the state and had always worked for the general good. Once a month, in his spare time, he'd meet with some friends—professors, school inspectors—and proofread translations of foreign books into the Khmer language. He didn't want to leave his country.

And he didn't think he was in any danger, even though he'd worked for every government through the years.

Using the sequence of events in China as an example, he assured us he would no doubt be sent to a reeducation camp for a while; such an outcome seemed to him to be practically in the natural order of things. Then conditions would start to improve. He believed in his usefulness to the country, and in social justice. As for my mother and us, the children, the Khmer Rouge wouldn't consider us important. That, then, was the analysis of an educated, well-informed man, a man with peasant origins to boot. In retrospect it's easy to see the naïveté in his assessment. His viewpoint was, first and foremost, that of a humanist, a progressive who envisioned a humanistic revolution.

However, my father knew that some acts of violence had already occurred. Around the end of 1971 a schoolteacher had explained to him that teaching in the zones occupied by the Khmer Rouge insurgents was almost impossible. He spoke of extortion, torture, murder. They were pitiless, he said, and most of all there seemed to be nothing in their organization that was either egalitarian or free.

The popular revolution was cruel, but on the other hand Lon Nol's regime was no better, with its trail of disappearances and arbitrary executions. The peasants would no longer put up with destitution and servitude. Their misery was increased by the American bombardments in the hinterlands. In the towns, too, the ruling power was loathed; in a climate of penury, corruption had reached intolerable levels. It was on this fertile ground of anger that the Khmer Rouge, with their discipline, their ideology, and their dialectics, had prospered.

My father had met Ieng Sary after his return from France in the mid-1950s. Ieng Sary had gone on to become an important Khmer Rouge leader, and then in 1963 he'd disappeared into the jungle with Pol Pot. At that time my father had helped his wife. Their children were in the same school as we were. My father couldn't imagine this former pupil in the Lycée Condorcet, this student of Marx, this professor of history and geography, participating in an inhuman or criminal enterprise. He figured that the new regime would make educating the masses a priority. Basically he had faith in his own program.

The French protectorate of Cambodia had come to an end in 1953, but true independence is not so easily obtained. Under Lon Nol's regime propaganda was everywhere. A climate of violence prevailed. Like all boys of my age I was fascinated by the rifles and the uniforms. Whenever a military truck approached our house, I'd station myself outside with a wooden gun. I drew tanks in my notebooks.

When I reflect on the situation, I feel certain that children in the countryside must have shared the same fascination, but the Khmer Rouge took them in hand very early, at eleven or twelve years old. They were given a uniform—black shirt, black pants, a traditional checkered scarf (a *krama*), a pair of sandals cut from tire rubber—a rifle, and, above all, an ironclad ideal and an iron discipline. What would I have thought if someone had consigned a weapon to me and promised a people's revolution that would bring equality, fraternity, justice? I would have been happy, as one is when he believes.

THE FIGHTING WAS getting closer to Phnom Penh. We could feel the earth shaking from the American bombardments: the famous "carpet bombing" strategy already employed in Vietnam. My country cousins had warned me that when the B-52s approached, I shouldn't throw myself flat on the ground; the vibrations in the earth could give you ear- and nosebleeds, even at a distance of several hundred yards. They also taught me to recognize the whistling of rockets. They couldn't take being hungry and thirsty and afraid anymore. Because of the air raids, they had to harvest their fields at night. They all died alongside the Khmer Rouge. That's not hard to explain: the more bombs the American B-52s dropped, the more peasants joined the revolution, and the more territory the Khmer Rouge gained.

The refugees crowded into the capital. They seemed dazed. Rationing became widespread. There were shortages of water, rice, electricity, gasoline. We took in my aunt and her two children and lodged them on the ground floor of our house. We could hear the rockets whistling as they fell on our neighborhood, and then the mournful wailing of the ambulance sirens. My school was located across from a pagoda, so we witnessed, with increasing frequency, the cremations of officers who had died in combat. A general, impalpable atmosphere of anxiety pervaded the city. We were waiting, but for what? Freedom? Revolution? I couldn't recognize anyone anymore— all faces were closed. It was then that I put away my wooden rifle. The party was over, and I had no ideal to aspire to.

ON APRIL 17 my family, like all the other inhabitants of the capital, converged on the city center. I remember that my sister was driving without a license. They're coming! They're coming! We wanted to be there, to see, to understand, to participate. There was already a rumor afoot that we were going to be evacuated. People ran behind the columns of armed men, all of them dressed in black. They were young, old, and in between, and like all peasants, they wore their pants rolled up to their knees.

Many books declare that Phnom Penh joyously celebrated the arrival of the revolutionaries. I recall instead feverishness, disquiet, a sort of anguished fear of the unknown. And I don't remember any scenes of fraternization. What surprised us was that the revolutionaries didn't smile. They kept us at a distance, coldly. I quickly noticed the looks in their eyes, their clenched jaws, their fingers on their triggers. I was frightened by that first encounter, by the entire absence of feeling.

SOME YEARS AGO I met and filmed a former Khmer Rouge soldier, a member of an elite unit, who confirmed to me that they'd received clear instructions on the eve of the great day: "Don't touch anyone. No one at all. And if you have no choice, never touch a person with your hand; use your rifle barrel."

ANNOTATION IN RED INK in the register of S-21, across from the names of three young children: "Grind them into dust." Signature: "Duch." Duch acknowledges that it's his handwriting. Yes, he's the one who wrote that. But he clarifies his statement: he wrote those words at the request of his deputy, Comrade Hor, the head of the security unit, in order to "jolt" Comrade Peng, who seemed to be hesitating.

The pages of that register each contain between twenty and thirty names. Accompanying every name, Duch jotted a note in his own hand—"Destroy." "Keep." "Can be destroyed." "Photograph needed."—as though he had detailed knowledge of each case. The thoroughness of torture. The thoroughness of the work of torture.

WE WENT TO STAY with friends who gave us temporary lodging in the center of the capital. At an intersection jammed with vehicles, soldiers, and a crowd of people, a Khmer Rouge commander riding in a jeep with a pistol at his belt and a cohort of bodyguards around him recognized my father, put his hands together in greeting, and slowly bowed. Who was he? A former pupil? A schoolteacher? A peasant from my father's native village? A few yards farther on my father said to my sister, "Let's try over to the right," but at once he received a violent blow to the temple from a rifle butt. "No! To the left!" a young Khmer Rouge yelled. We obeyed him.

When my older sister's husband, who was a surgeon, saw what terrible shape the refugees were in, the pregnant women on the roads, the gravely ill abandoned to their fate, he left us and went back to the Khmer-Soviet Friendship Hospital. For days on end he performed operations and provided medical care, and then he was evacuated, together with all the patients. The chaos was indescribable. And there were no longer any means of communication—or rather communication itself was forbidden. My brother-in-law searched in vain for us and then set out alone for his native province. Fifteen years later I learned that he'd been arrested at Taing Kauk. Somebody recognized him and denounced him as a physician. At that time people would make denunciations for a bowl of rice. Or out of revenge. Or jealousy. Or to ingratiate themselves with the new power. A physician? He was executed on the spot.

About a year later his wife, my elder sister, disappeared. Both of them, she and her husband, had worked for Cambodia. What could be better than archaeology and medicine? The body of the past and the living body? My father had hesitated too long to send them to France, even though a grant would have made it possible, and even though he'd already succeeded in sending four of his children abroad. He wanted them to specialize, to make further progress, and then to come back and serve their country. But he gave up the idea.

When I go to the archaeological museum—the National Museum of Cambodia, a complex of red buildings with ornate, soaring roofs, built by the French—I think about my sister, who, despite her young age, was the museum's deputy director. When I was eight or nine years old, I often went to visit her in her office. I'd climb up on the little brick wall and use a stick to knock down fruit from the big tamarind trees. The ripe tamarinds were delicious. Today I wouldn't dare do that. Because of my age? Or my memories? The royal palace, with its high walls and its traditions, isn't far. The world we knew will not return. And you, my sister, I never saw you again. I can still picture your colorful skirt when you would appear at the big, carved wooden door, and your bag filled with documents. I remember our walks together. Your words. And my caprices. I see you smile. You take my childish hand.

EARLY ON THE MORNING of April 17, a soldier presented himself at our front door: "Take your things! Leave the house! Right away!" We sprang into action. Immediately, without knowing why or how, we obeyed. Did we already feel fear? I don't think so. It was more like astonishment. One of our neighbors, a handyman who'd become a Khmer Rouge commander, tried to reassure us.

The whole city was in the streets. The men in black told us we'd be back in two or three days. The hunt for traitors and enemies had begun. The purge was hideous but classic in those circumstances. The Khmer Rouge were looking for army officers, senior civil servants, supporters of Lon Nol. According to a spreading rumor, the Americans were going to bomb the capital. The Khmer Rouge leaders had frequently alluded to the possibility of an American bombing, and then certain Western intellectuals had echoed the speculation. The Americans did nothing. Who could have seriously entertained the thought that they would bomb a city of two million people just a few days after withdrawing their personnel and ending their support? I still remember the helicopters evacuating their embassy. You needed a lot of hatred and a good deal of blindness, or some unspeakable other reason, to believe in that fable.

Each of us carried a bag prepared by my mother, with her innate practical sense, and we left in the car. We didn't get very far. Before long we were lost in the human flood.

There were women and children pushing wheelbarrows, men carrying insanely heavy loads, people half-crazed—and everywhere the fifteen-year-old fighters, with their cold eyes, their black uniforms, and the cartridges in their bandoliers.

Historians today think that the revolutionaries drove some 40 percent of Cambodia's total population into the countryside. In the course of a few days. There was no overall plan. No organization. No dispositions had been made to guide, feed, care for, or lodge those thousands and thousands of people. Gradually we began to see sick people on the roads, old folks, serious invalids, stretchers. We sensed that the evacuation was turning bad. Fear was palpable.

I QUESTION DUCH tirelessly. Although he looks the tribunal's prosecutors, judges, and attorneys in the eye—he has a monitor in front of him and knows when he's being filmed—he never gazes into my camera. Or hardly ever. Is he afraid it will see inside him?

Duch talks to heaven, which in this case is a white ceiling. He explains his position to me. He makes phrases. I catch him lying. I offer precise information. He hesitates. When in a difficult situation, Duch rubs his face with his damaged hand. He breathes loudly. He massages his forehead and his eyelids, and then he examines the neon lighting.

One day during a dialogue that's turning into a fight, I see the skin of his cheeks grow blotchy. I stare at his irritated, bristling flesh. Then his calm returns, the soldier's calm, the calm of the revolutionary who's had to face so many cruel committees and endure so many self-criticism sessions. Then I stop filming him and say, "Think about it; take your time."

He smiles and speaks softly to me, "Mr. Rithy, we won't quarrel tomorrow, will we?" I see clearly that he'd like us to understand each other and laugh together. And he needs to talk to me. To continue the discussion. To win me over. No, he's no monster, and he's even less of a demon. He's a man who searches out and seizes upon the weaknesses of others. A man who stalks his humanity. A disturbing man. I don't remember that he ever left me without a laugh or a smile.

WE DROVE SEVERAL MILES and stopped. Should we go on? Where? A soldier walked up and, without a word, signaled that we should get moving again. My father sighed and clenched his fists. The scene was repeated twice more. The Khmer Rouge spoke a rather odd language, using words I knew little or not at all. For example, they used the verb *snœur* to confiscate our car, which they later left on the side of the road. Theoretically *snœur* means "to ask politely." The word was smooth, almost soft, but the look in the eyes was violent. Thirty years later Duch evokes Stalin, "an iron fist in a velvet glove," and summarizes the Khmer Rouge attitude this way: "courteous but firm."

This way of speaking made us uneasy. If words lose their meaning, what's left of us? For the first time, I heard a reference to the Angkar (the "Organization"), which has filled up my life ever since. We set out on foot, and then the sun sank behind the rice fields.

We were beginning to guess, from the tone and looks of the Khmer Rouge, that we wouldn't be seeing Phnom Penh again anytime soon. And I don't remember encountering anywhere the force, the joyful excitement, or the freedom of the first sansculottes.

IN M-13, DUCH frequently attended interrogations. He reflected upon them. Observed them carefully. "I went so far as to derive a theory from them," he tells me. I don't understand this formulation. "Derive a theory from them? What theory? Explain it to me . . ." He replies, "I remained polite but firm." Then he falls silent.

THE SECOND NIGHT, my mother asked my father to go and throw away his neckties. The searches hadn't started yet, but rumor had it that some young people with long hair had been executed and their heads paraded around on staffs. My father disappeared into the forest, ties in hand, and came back after hiding his former life.

AT DAWN ON THE DAY after the fall of Phnom Penh, the prisoners inside M-13 prison, in the northern part of the country, received an order to start digging. Under the white-hot sky, sweating and suffering, they excavated a ditch. How many of them were there? Dozens? We'll never know. They were executed. Nothing remains of those mass graves, some of which may have been immense. As the years passed, the Khmer Rouge planted cassava root and coconut palms, which have since consumed bodies and memory.

Duch reached Phnom Penh with his entire crew: several dozen peasants—a few as young as thirteen or fourteen— whom he'd chosen and then educated in the ways of torture. Duch's team included Tuy, Tith, Pon, and Mam Nay, known as Chan. Some of these men were also former professors. Mam Nay had been in prison with Duch, his friend, his double. They both spoke French fluently, and they had an almost intuitive mutual understanding.

The new history had begun; the murderers were waiting in the outskirts of the capital. Soon they would occupy the former Ponhea Yat lycée, which would be known as S-21.

Later I show Duch a photograph of Bophana before she was tortured. Black eyes, black hair. She seems impassive. Already elsewhere. He holds the photo a long time. "Looking at this document disturbs me," he says. He seems moved. Is it compassion? Is it memory? Is it his own emotion that touches him? He's silent again for a while, and then he concludes, "We're all under the sky. When it rains, who doesn't get wet?"

WE ADOPTED THE HABIT of sleeping in the forest, not far from the road. We'd throw a plastic sheet on the ground and lie down on it.

Most necessities were unobtainable: drinking water, milk for the babies, medical assistance, fire. Prices sky-rocketed. For my thirteenth birthday on April 18, my mother had bought a ham on the sly and had it caramelized. It must have cost tens of thousands of riels. We shared that dish, but I don't think any of us smiled during the meal.

After a few days the rumor started going around that our currency wasn't worth anything anymore, that it was simply going to disappear. Vendors started refusing to take banknotes. The effect was devastating. How could we eat, how could we drink, how could we live without money? Bartering had sprung up again as soon as the evacuation began, and now it was widespread. The rich became poorer; the poor stripped themselves bare. Money's not merely violence—it also dissolves; it divides. Barter affirms what's absolutely lacking and renders the fragile more fragile still.

My provident mother had brought away with us a quantity of sheets, which she exchanged for food. Those big pieces of fabric were very useful. My mother was able to obtain some mess tins, some American army spoons, a bucket, a pan, and a boiling kettle so that we could drink, risk-free, water from the Bassak River.

We came to realize that this trend was irreversible.

Years later I looked at some extraordinary archival photographs; they show the Central Bank of Cambodia right after the revolutionaries blew it up. Only the corners of the building remain, sad pieces of metal-reinforced lacework standing over rubble. The message is clear. There's no treasure; there are no riches that can't be annihilated. We'll dynamite our old world, and thus we'll prove that capitalism is but dust inside four walls.

A lovely program, worth a minute's consideration. It's often the case, in every country, that rebels call for a society without currency. Is it the money that disgusts them? Or the desire to consume that it reveals? Exchange is supposed to have unrecognized capabilities. Free exchange, which is the term used for barter. But I've never seen a free exchange. A gift is something else. I lived for four years in a society without currency, and I never felt that the absence of money made injustice easier to bear. And I can't forget that the very idea of value had disappeared. Nothing could be estimated, or esteemed, anymore—not human life or anything else. But to assess something, to evaluate it, doesn't necessarily mean to have contempt for it or to destroy it.

Nothing could be assessed anymore? Well not exactly nothing, because throughout that whole period, gold never stopped discreetly circulating. It had extraordinary power. With gold you could cause what had disappeared to appear again—penicillin, for example. Rice, sugar, tobacco. The Khmer Rouge were full participants in such trafficking.

Other archival images: the treasury. Nailed wooden crates, discovered in a warehouse. Inside, under sheets of transparent plastic, the official banknotes of the new country. So it seems that Democratic Kampuchea had its currency ready to circulate after all. What happened? Logistical problems? Further doctrinal radicalization? The new currency was never used.

We bartered what we could—in the beginning, exchanges of that sort were tolerated—but very soon, we had nothing left to exchange. Contrary to the popular notion, it's not true that there's always "something left" to swap. I've seen a country stripped completely bare, where a fork was a possession too precious to give away, where a hammock was a treasure. Nothing's more real than nothing.

I CAN THINK of few examples in contemporary history of a population transfer so massive and so sudden. What to call it? Organized exodus? Forced march? I don't want to be told that the Khmer Rouge had no choice, that they were at war with everyone, that they'd just come out of the jungle, that they had no human or technical resources, that they did their best in a troubled time, or that it's easy to be right in hindsight. I don't want to hear that the Khmer Rouge acted as they did because they thought it would be a solution to the impending famine they claimed to dread the prospect of. Or that the American bombers were already circling over the capital.

Unfortunately I can't see in the "evacuation of Phnom Penh" anything other than the beginning of the extermination of the "new people," namely—according to Duch's own definition—"capitalists, landlords, civil servants, members of the middle class, intellectuals, professors, students." The cities and therefore the universities, the libraries, the cinemas, the courts, and the administrative offices were to be emptied. Those centers of commerce, of corruption, of debauchery, of every sort of trafficking were to be emptied. Hospitals and clinics were to be emptied too. The evacuation of the capital prefigured the overall plan that we now know was in place.

The first political decision of the new order was to shake up the society: to uproot city dwellers; to dissolve families; to put an end to all previous activities, especially professional activities; to break with political, intellectual, and cultural traditions; to weaken individuals physically and psychologically. The forced evacuations took place at the same time all over the country, and no cities were excepted.

And so the complete overthrow of society began. Very quickly, as one may imagine, there were thousands of deaths and a great many sick and starving people.

Now let's reason in the opposite direction. Let's take as our hypothesis that the Khmer Rouge wanted to *protect* the inhabitants of the cities in general and of Phnom Penh in particular. Once the "political cleansing" (I don't know what else to call that manhunt) and the American bombardments were over, why didn't they organize the return of the population? It wouldn't have been simple, of course, but tens of thousands of deaths could have been avoided. The hypothesis is, unfortunately, absurd. Why would the revolutionaries protect members of the class they hated? In fact, right up to the end, they never stopped undermining, starving, "forging," and exterminating the "bourgeoisie." The Khmer Rouge leaders' overall plan was nothing if not consistent. And they got what they wanted: the almost immediate destruction of the middle class.

WELL BEFORE THOSE EVENTS, I remember my father taking me with him to visit a woman who was very close to the revolutionaries. I called her Aunt Tha. She and her husband, Uch Ven, had studied in France and then returned to Cambodia. Shortly thereafter he'd gone underground

and become an important figure in the insurgent movement. He died of malaria, Duch informed me.

His wife lived in Phnom Penh with their children. I
liked to go to visit her because they had an electric train.
The police had her under constant surveillance. Nothing
in her past or present seemed to trouble my father. He ap-
preciated the woman—her intelligence, her life story, her
courage—and she was a frequent guest in our home. She
was like one of the family.

Much later I met one of my father's former pupils, who
said to me, "Ah, you're Panh Lauv's son! He was a demand-
ing teacher, but he was fantastic . . ." he said. And then he
told me this story: once, back when he was a pupil, he'd
had a pretty violent fight with a rich kid in the schoolyard.
The other boy's father came to the school administration
to complain, and my father reassured him, telling him,
"Don't worry, it won't happen again. I'm going to fix the
problem." As he spoke, he picked up a rattan cane and
brandished it with a martial air. The important man and
his son left, no doubt gratified by the thought of what
awaited the other pupil. My father sought him out and
said, "You were right to give that insufferable rich kid a
couple of good whacks. He's too stupid, and so is his father. But watch yourself; otherwise you're going to have
problems. I'm not going to hit you in any case! Now run
on home." And that was the end of that.

I ASK DUCH about the famine that consumed the country, beginning in 1975. "As far as the famine was concerned, I was informed. I knew about it. My mother came to see me," Duch smiles. "And she was suffering from hunger too." I point out that his mother lived in Kampong Thom, and that it would have been impossible for her to get to Phnom Penh by car or truck; all movement was strictly forbidden. Moreover there was nothing left in the capital but the government, the administration, a few embassies whose personnel were sequestered, a few rare factories, and S-21 prison. Nothing could approach that vast, secret complex.

Duch continues: "How could I help my mother?" He laughs again. "If I gave her some rice, I'd be arrested." Notice that last statement: giving your mother rice was a crime. But traveling all the way across the country to see your son and complain to him—wasn't that a crime too?

I reply, "Your mother crossed the country to visit you in S-21? You're joking."

"Not at all. She knew everybody."

"Mr. Duch, everybody knew *you*!"

He says he subsequently wrote a report on the famine for his first boss, Son Sen, a member of the Central Committee of the Communist Party, Democratic Kampuchea's minister of defense, and the head of the Party's security apparatus. By mentioning this report, Duch affirms his humanity and his solidarity with his suffering fellow Cambodians. The famine spared no one. Even Duch's mother was a victim.

Son Sen's answer to Duch's report was as follows: "Of course! She's right. It's the enemy that's starving the people. It's the enemy we haven't stopped completely."

And Duch comments, "At the time, everyone believed that."

No confession is ever stated clearly and directly. It comes in a murmur that requires careful attention on the part of the listener. I put his last sentence into logical form: "At the time, everyone believed that the enemy was starving us and that if we stopped him, we wouldn't be hungry anymore. That wasn't true. It wasn't true, but we, we the Khmer Rouge, lied to ourselves. And we believed our lie." At his level of responsibility—he was the regime's chief of police, as he himself says—Duch couldn't have been unaware of that lie. I insist on the "we," the first-person plural, because Duch always says "they" when he's talking about the Khmer Rouge. "They didn't think about people's lives," he'll say. They are not him. The revolutionary is the other guy.

DURING OUR CONVERSATION, Duch makes a marvelously inhuman remark, but does he know it? He says, "It's not me who doesn't have a mother." And he laughs.

My family on the road: my parents, my oldest sister, my two unmarried sisters, my three young nephews, and me. Phal, a boy two years my senior who'd been living in our house for several months, accompanied us. He was a poor orphan whom my parents, in accordance with Cambodian tradition, had taken in; they were feeding him, clothing him, and giving him a proper upbringing. Phal did his share of the household chores. We all took turns collecting eggs, feeding the ducks and the dogs, washing the floor, and doing the laundry. This was only to be expected in a house where some fifteen people lived.

We stopped for two days in a pagoda at Koh Thom, not far from an immense automobile graveyard where displaced persons had abandoned their vehicles. We were shut up inside the pagoda, and it was there that the first count was made. (After that the counts never stopped.) How many of us were there? Where did our family come from? What was my father's profession? The Khmer Rouge were insistent, almost aggressive.

Then—together with our luggage, which seemed to be getting heavier and heavier—we were put on a boat at night, and we approached the Vietnamese frontier. Phnom Penh was far away.

WE DISEMBARKED at a pagoda in Koh Tauch. Everything was mysterious. Up until then the idea of Buddhist monks engaged in rice production would have been unthinkable, but bonzes from that pagoda were hard at work in the paddies. Others were being consulted by all sorts of people. We learned that a general was under house arrest. We could barely make out his silhouette. He seemed immobile. Then he disappeared, having been "taken away to study." It was the first time we'd heard this expression, and we honestly thought it referred to reeducation.

EVERY INSTANT IS CRUEL. One evening the Khmer Rouge demand that we unpack our baggage. Without a word we spread out all our things, flat on the ground and spaced well apart. The Khmer Rouge want to know who we are. They find no document, no sign of collaboration with the enemy. There are some pieces of fabric, a few jewels, and some money, which they don't even take. One of them shrugs his shoulders and barks at us, "This is all over, this stuff." Money, all over? We're amazed.

I haven't forgotten their stares when they came across my sisters' brassieres. The fifteen-year-old child soldiers were like men. And we were, so to speak, naked.

One of them took apart a little notebook in which my sister had glued various souvenirs and removed an old visiting card. He showed it to us without a word: "Panh Lauv, Chief Undersecretary, Ministry of National Education." The card even showed his telephone number—much more compromising than a bunch of neckties. We were terrified.

THEN WE WERE TURNED OVER to a family of "old people." An elderly couple took us into their house, which was built on stilts. Two of my sisters, who were above the age of fourteen, left to live in a "youth group." With Phal, but also with the old couple's son-in-law, a Khmer Rouge, I discovered peasant life. I didn't know how to do anything. Nothing at all. I didn't know how to fish or identify edible roots or unearth a snail. I couldn't even row. I discovered a harsh world where you had to plunge into cold water bristling with reeds, feel around the muddy bottom, and empty the fish traps. We planted rice, corn, and cassava root.

Phal suffered from terrible attacks of diarrhea, one of which nearly killed him in the course of a few hours. I can still remember my eldest sister washing his soiled pants in the river several times a day. He couldn't control himself. We were close, the two of us, and I was very sad, but he finally recovered.

Phal was familiar with peasant life, and so he gained a sort of ascendancy. We'd both begun to frequent the evening study groups organized by the Khmer Rouge. Topics of discussion: the class struggle, its procession of injustices, and revolution. In a month Phal changed. He became bitter. His consciousness had been raised. Or was it his resentment? He went to the person in charge of the village and explained that he'd been mistreated, that my parents were slave drivers, that they should be punished. The man jotted down everything in his notebook.

We have to believe that the revolutionary movement wasn't so radical early on because Phal got himself bawled out by the old man who owned the house we stayed in: "This is the way you treat your family? Look at your sister, who washes your clothes when they're drenched in shit! And the way everyone takes care of you! You ought to be ashamed of yourself!" Later on talking like that would become inconceivable.

I WATCHED the countryside being carried off by the gigantic Bassac River. Its flooding waters, muddy and lugubrious, reached the edge of the forest. That river was the center of our existence. The school year was lost, but my father was apparently the only one of us who still gave any thought to that.

MY MOTHER received permission to stay in the house and take care of my young nephew and niece. Because I was only thirteen, I was allowed to remain with my parents. The old man entrusted his oxen to me. Those enormous beasts, which would breathe down my neck and come to sudden stops for no reason at all, made me uncomfortable. I'd speak to them. I'd implore them. They would disregard me like divinities gazing dry-eyed upon the earth. A child told me I should stay behind them and strike them with a stick. When I did so, they'd start to move again, stirring up the air with their dirty tails. They'd plow in the morning, and then around noon, I'd lead them to the low forest, where they could stay cool. In the evening, I'd go back to the cowshed and make a fire of twigs and peat to chase away the mosquitoes. Then I'd collapse on a mat. Still today I can feel my mother's hand stroking my forehead.

I ALSO CROSSED a branch of the gigantic river, suffocated by whirlwinds of mud, with one hand on an ox's halter and the other on his ear. Then a peasant's son explained to me the only feasible method: grab a beast's tail and let myself be pulled along, taking care to avoid being struck by a hoof.

We were in the service of the cooperative, but our lives weren't entirely communal. I ate my meals, for example, with my family—my parents and my niece and nephew—and no one else. When a pig was slaughtered each family in attendance would be called by name and given a bit of fat. Food distribution always took place in two stages: first came the "new people," who were quickly provided for, and then the "old people." The quantity and quality of the meat you got depended on the category you belonged to. Money was still refusing to disappear, and some among us were dreaming of becoming millionaires. "New people" could use jewelry or fabrics to negotiate with "old people." A kilogram of pork cost hundreds of thousands of riels. Then everything stopped.

The atmosphere of those first months, as I perceived it, was characterized more by distrust than by fear. Everything surprised me. But the revolution hadn't yet reached its radical phase, or to be more precise, its terror phase.

Around the same time, we received some sacks of hard corn, an official gift from our Chinese comrades. The kernels were huge, pale, and infested by insects. In the old days, such corn was usually fed to pigs, but we picked over those kernels, one by one. A peasant who saw how hungry I was offered me some dog. A man eats a dog, I thought. What an idea.

Two friends and I spotted a peninsula, and I swam out to it. I found fish and shellfish there: a treasure! I tied my catch around my neck and swam back, nearly drowning from sheer fatigue in the process. The river was ferrying along parts of trees, great blocks of earth, exhausted animals . . . Why deny it? It was an adventure. I discovered peasant life in all its harshness and power. I learned to lay traps and to smoke tobacco wrapped in *sangker* leaves, just as the children of the "old people" did. I said to myself, "Will my friends in Phnom Penh believe me when I tell them about all this? When I describe how I caught fish with my bare hands?" I was already thinking about telling my story. The road has been long, and I doubt that "my friends in Phnom Penh" are still alive.

Soon the prohibitions and vexations began to multiply. Communal living grew harder. The "old people" ate well and spoke harshly to us.

One morning I saw a harrowing sight: a swollen corpse floating on the river. I thought about the famine and all the fighting. Weeks passed. More bodies appeared in the river. Some of them got caught on steel-hard roots near the bank. We went closer. There was no blood, but the bodies had large purple bruises and deep cuts. Those men and women had been executed.

Revolutions are hungry. The prospect of telling my great adventure story began to fade in my mind, as did the hope of returning to my former life.

WE ENDED UP sleeping in the old couple's house, right beside them. I remember that they prayed to Buddha and their ancestors at night, but they didn't dare burn incense. Militiamen hid under the bamboo floor to listen in on our conversations. They heard my father wondering about Ieng Sary. Where was he now? Was he aware of the turn the revolution was taking? Would the two of them meet again? That celebrated name petrified the Khmer Rouge, who spared my parents.

The cold season came, heralded by the north wind and the subsidence of the big river. I gazed hungrily upon several kilos of fish in an enormous bomb crater, a souvenir from the B-52 bombardments, but I couldn't catch any of them. I didn't have the strength. I went home in tears, trembling with fever and staggering in the clayey mud.

The rice ripened, the cassava matured, and all the plants gave their fruits. But the Angkar decided that we had to leave. So we went on foot from Koh Tauch to where a motor boat was waiting for us, and we were taken to the other bank of the Bassac.

THE KHMER ROUGE used many terms I didn't recognize. Frequently these were invented words based on existing ones; they mixed up sounds and meanings in disconcerting ways. Everything seemed to glide. To slip: Why did they use *santebal*, not the traditional word *nokorbal*, to designate the police? Another new word I discovered was *kamaphibal*. *Kamak* may be translated as "activity" or "action"—a *kamakor* is a worker—and *phibal* means "guard." Literally a *kamaphibal* was a "guard of work," a "guard of action." The word denoted members of the Khmer Rouge cadres, who were our masters and jailers and had over us the power of life and death.

ONE NIGHT ABOUT twenty trucks appeared. The Khmer Rouge made many families, including mine, climb into these vehicles. The drivers, who were very young, didn't speak to us. We drove into the suburbs of Phnom Penh. Everything looked empty. But many of the passengers in the trucks rejoiced, thinking they were going to return to their homes and—why not?—their former lives.

The convoy of trucks made a sudden turn. I remember an old man gazing at the stars and murmuring, "We're going away from the city." Then we fell silent. We were hungry and thirsty. The truck we rode in rattled along a dirt road that seemed to have no end. It stopped at last in the middle of the rice fields. The trucks discharged their passengers—the air was heavy with dust and gasoline vapors—and the convoy drove off. I tried to make out a village or some kind of shelter, but in vain. Nothing. The old people, the women, and we children sat down on the road. You could hear people murmuring and sighing. Nobody dared to speak. From time to time a Khmer Rouge came out of nowhere, made sure we were all there, and left without a word.

I remember the night was starry. Rustling, hissing, croaking sounds rose up from all around us. The countryside seemed to be in heat. And I couldn't sleep.

Then the terrible sun began to climb the sky. We still didn't know what was going on. A soldier brought us some bread and left us there in the middle of the immense rice field. A few days later, we got into some cattle cars in a rail yard. The doors slid closed with a metallic sound, and the train headed north. We were all on our feet and packed in tight. After several silent, exhausting hours I had the impression I could see into the darkness. The train kept stopping for no apparent reason. We'd wait alongside the tracks in the middle of the night. Some people started to cook a little rice, but a man shouted an order, we climbed back into the cars in a panic, and the train set out again.

THE TRAIN EVENTUALLY let us off near Mong, in the northwest part of the country. My mother handed Phal his bag and said simply, "It's over now. Be on your way." He begged us to keep him. It was horrible. He became a child again. He implored my mother, wringing his hands, but she remained inflexible. He'd betrayed us at a difficult moment; she couldn't forgive him. Moreover she sensed that the worst was yet to come. We'd need to trust one another fully. And so he left. I can still see his tearful face, and then his silhouette disappearing into the night.

We climbed into some carts in which we bounced across the rice fields. It was an incredible trip, and at the end of it the Khmer Rouge ordered us out of the carts. It wasn't possible to go any farther. We sat down in some ditches. When the dawn came we could see a stony, arid plain and an oasis of mango trees with a border of bamboo. We walked to a house, which belonged to the "old people" who would be in charge of us. We had to build everything, or almost everything, together with the few persons who seemed to be living there already. We were forbidden to use the well. The water in the canal was brown, and many of us fell sick.

We searched in vain for rice. The famine was getting worse. The authorities began to distribute bowls of lukewarm broth with green threads floating in it. That was our daily meal.

STARVATION IS THE PREMIER mass crime, always so difficult to establish with certainty, as if its very causes have been eaten up. Stalin starved his peasants by the millions. He persecuted his elites. His generals, his doctors, his friends, his relations, his family. Massacres are part of revolutions. Those who call for society to be upended know this fact very well and never condemn violence. Their argument is always the same: only new violence can drive out previous violence. The previous violence is hideous and cruel. The new violence is pure and beneficent; it transforms (not to say transfigures). It's not violence aimed at an individual; it's a political act. And blood purifies. I'll come back to the Angkar's slogan, which Duch so admired: "The blood debt must be repaid by blood."

For an identifiable reason or no reason at all, the purges swoop down on some and leave others alone. They're impossible to stop. The doctrines change, and so do the hands, but there's always a blade and a guilty throat to cut in the name of justice, in the name of safeguarding the regime, in the name of some name. In the name of "proletarian morale," Duch says. In the name of nothing: if a throat is slit, that in itself indicates the presence of some fault. Much is attributed to great criminals, and the following extraordinary statement is attributed to Stalin: "No people, no problems."

The name of the man who sponsored Duch's entrance into the clandestine Communist Party in the middle of the 1960s was Ker Pauk. He was notoriously violent. It's known that he carried out mass executions. That he threw living Cambodians down wells. It was his troops who arrested Bophana. He was known as the "Great Butcher."

THE KHMER ROUGE observed us constantly. They noticed my slender fingers. One of them snapped at me, "You've got bourgeois fingers. You've never held a hoe!" I'm a "new people"; I have a "new people's" body; my new body, therefore, needs work. But hard labor, injuries, calluses change nothing. My fingers are still too slender. So I move away from the front rows. I learn to hide my hands, to clench my fists, to melt away, to disappear.

DURING OUR INTERVIEWS, I was amazed to see how re-
laxed and attentive Duch was. He was an extremely calm
man, however inhumane his crimes might have been.
One could have imagined he'd forgotten them. Or that
he hadn't committed them. The question today is not to
find out whether he's human or not. He's human at every
instant; that's the reason why he can be judged and condemned. No one can rightly authorize himself to human-
ize or dehumanize anyone. But no one can occupy *Duch's
place* in the human community. No one can duplicate his
biographical, intellectual, and psychological trajectory. No
one can believe he was a cog among other cogs in the killing machine. I'll return later to the contemporary notion
that we're all potential torturers. This fatalism tinged with
smugness exercises literature, film, and certain intellectuals. After all what's more exciting than a great criminal?
No, we're not all a fraction of an inch, the depth of a sheet
of paper, from committing a great crime. For my part I
believe in facts and I look at the world. The victims are in
their place. The torturers too.

MY FATHER WAS tall and straight. With his broad forehead
and piercing eyes, he impressed others. Whatever the season (I'm referring to the time of the former regime, of
course, the time before 1975), he wore a white shirt, cuff

links, a tie, and a double-breasted suit, required attire in the ministries. French had remained the language used in his line of work.

He smoked a lot, and I loved bringing him his metal cigarette case. I used to light his last cigarette of the day. I remember him like that, smoking pensively. My mother would sit beside him, lost in the clouds of his smoke, and read the newspaper.

Sometimes he'd come to visit me at school and get into discussions with the principal. I'd keep my distance, a bit frightened by those serious men who seemed to have so much to say to each other. From time to time, my father would show up to watch my tae kwon do training sessions. He'd lean against a tree, silent, attentive, with half-closed eyes. I was proud of him. Proud of his presence, proud of his gaze. He'd smile at me before he disappeared.

He was born into a peasant family struggling to survive on the Cambodian-Vietnamese border in the 1920s. There were nine or ten children. Everything's uncertain in the rich earth of the rice fields, where bones can bleach white in a year. For such peasants as those, there was no civil status and no history; there was nothing but the tallying of hours and animals.

But my father's fate was different, special, because his own father chose him to receive an education. Why him and not one of his siblings? It's a mystery. His brothers and sisters were in the fields, planting rice or tending flocks, while he was going to school in Phnom Penh. He never spoke to me about that period of his life, but he must have felt both happy and completely alone in the capital, where his fellow pupils laughed at his shabby clothes.

He became a teacher, then a primary school inspector, and then, for nearly ten years, the chief undersecretary in the Ministry of Education. He read a great deal—newspapers, magazines, books. Not to mention the innumerable files and documents that would sometimes be brought to the house, late in the evening, for him to sign. He liked debates, but he also liked quiet reflection. I know he would have wished to make greater progress in various fields of knowledge, no easy task when you've started out as a poor peasant from the borderlands and you've got nine kids yourself.

Education was what he fought for. He admired Jules Ferry and the French public school system. His guiding principle, the idea that obsessed him, was that there can be no economic and social development without education. It was a position from which he never budged. He was a purist, to the point of naïveté.

My father was a success in his way, but the material life didn't interest him. Steel rods protruded from the piers and the roof of our house. He couldn't have cared less; he lived for his profession. Soon after the Khmer Rouge takeover he lost the right to wear eyeglasses. Education now counted for nothing, except in propaganda. The world had changed; his world was gone.

I GAZE AT HIS FACE. At something over thirty he's smiling, looking frail in his black shirt; in a shot with his family he's hollow-featured, standing beside Mam Nay with a pen in his pocket; in a recent shot he's derisive, with one finger raised. I write in my notebook his various names and surnames: Yun Cheav, Kang Cheav, Keav, Kaing Yun Cheav, Kaing Guek Eav, Doan, Hang Pin. I remember only one: Duch.

MY FATHER LIKED to recite poems in his impeccable French. How many times did I hear him murmur the opening lines of a poem by Jacques Prévert, *Cheveux noirs, cheveux noirs, caressés par les vagues* . . . ("Black hair, black hair, caressed by the waves . . ."), lines I didn't understand? Several years ago I found a printed version of the text and then lost it, as if only that disembodied hair, those orphan words, could remain. As if the killing fields had won, had overrun the country and carried off everything, even sweet songs. I'm painting an idealized portrait of my father, of course, but the moral strength he displayed in the face of the Khmer Rouge made a great impression on me. In our democratic societies a man who believes in democracy seems to us an ordinary man. Maybe even a dull man. So I keep his somewhat yellowed picture in front of me in my Paris office. Let there be a banality of good, and let it be powerful. That will be his victory.

I ATE PAPAYA roots, banana roots, dried cowhide. Yes, cowhide. Like the hero in *The Gold Rush*, who boils his shoes for a long time and cuts up the laces and the soles while avoiding the nails. I chewed that inedible hide for hours, chewed it until I couldn't chew anymore; my jaws were turning into leather and wood. But the grilled hide sure smelled like cow, and I kept chewing.

For weeks I ate only water spinach, which is also used for pig fodder. I was a starveling, an eater of scraps.

I remember seeing other archival images that showed pigs wandering around inside the National Library in Phnom Penh, which the Khmer Rouge had emptied of its holdings. The pigs were knocking over chairs and trampling the peelings they were supposed to eat. Pigs had replaced the books. And we were replacing the pigs.

MY FATHER GREW exhausted, physically and morally. The new regime had deprived him of his profession and his reason for living. Now he was someone who had to be reeducated. He didn't know anything. Worse: what he knew, he knew badly. Books and newspapers had disappeared, for the most part prohibited and burned. My father, therefore, had nothing left but his memory, that store of poetic and hollow words. As he was too weak to work in the fields or in dike-building, the Angkar assigned him to a wicker workshop. He sat cross-legged on the floor with other old folks, weaving osiers. He was bad at it. His fingers bled. His belt had been confiscated, so he used lianas to hold up his khaki trousers.

One of his friends, a man of royal blood, would come to visit him some evenings, and we'd hear the two of them conversing in French, which was strictly forbidden. Very soon this friend was sent to a concentration camp. Some months later I saw him again in the hospital in Battambang, where he died. Once his friend was gone my father started talking to himself, murmuring phrases I didn't understand, absorbed in language.

In former days he would speak French with my older brothers. Some of the expressions they used have stayed with me, and today they make me laugh; at the time, however, they upset me. So did the prince, when he held forth in front of large crowds. He didn't speak; he shouted. I remember my father, standing straight and silent in the half-light, listening to a broadcast on the radio. From time to time he sighed. I was six years old, and I stared at my stern father, smoking with his eyes half-closed and his ears cocked to the radio. I sensed that he disagreed with what he was hearing. Today I know: politics is a loud cry.

IT SEEMS TO ME that I'd already attained a kind of maturity, but I obviously wasn't prepared for such a violent upheaval. From one day to the next the schools disappeared. We were required to dye our clothes: Good-bye, bright shirts; farewell, sarongs printed with colorful flowers. Everything became dark brown, gray, or midnight blue. We used some kind of fruit with an oily pulp that turned water black. Our hands looked withered. Loose pajamas became the general uniform. The Khmer Rouge forbade wearing glasses and marrying for love. They outlawed some words: "wife," for example, or "husband," because of their sexual and bourgeois connotations. The Khmer Rouge inculcated us with their slogans: "If you have a revolutionary mindset, comrade, everything is possible!" We were endlessly taught the twelve revolutionary commandments. The first one was "You will love, honor, and serve the people, the workers, and peasants." The second one: "Wherever you go, you will serve the people with your whole heart and your whole mind." The long twelfth commandment included the following passage: "You will struggle, with determination and courage, against every enemy and every obstacle, prepared to sacrifice anything, including your life, for the people, the workers, the peasants, the Revolution, and the Angkar, without hesitation and without respite."

All the pronouns in the language were changed. What's more individualistic than a pronoun? What's more dangerous than an identity? Since there's no individual person, a single syllable will do. The Khmer Rouge also went after members of all religious orders. Schools and pagodas, with their solid walls, became torture centers, hospitals, or food depots. The "new people" were sent to the country, there to perform the hardest tasks and thus shed their former skin. All agricultural land was collectivized. The stated goal was to triple the annual production of rice by developing irrigation. All our thoughts, all our actions were guided by this principle: "three tons of rice per hectare," that is 1.4 tons per acre; for some particularly zealous managers, the principle was "five tons of rice per hectare," or 2.3 tons per acre. Those figures were a refrain, an obsession—and an impossible dream.

Democratic Kampuchea became a worksite: canals were dug, dikes were built, rivers were diverted. An immense famine ensued. The worksite, it appeared, was in fact a labor camp.

Everything was subordinated to the Angkar, the mysterious, all-powerful "Organization": social life, the law, intellectual life, the family sphere, romantic relationships, relations with friends. I know of no other example in history of such dominion, of a sovereignty almost abstract by virtue of being absolute: "There are no more sales, no more exchanges, no more complaints, no more whining; there's no more theft or looting and no more intellectual property." I don't know how to name that political regime— the word "regime" itself doesn't seem right. It was a state characterized by "*non habeas corpus.*" In that world I'm not an individual. I have no freedom, no thoughts, no origin, no inheritance, no rights: I have no more body. All I have is a duty, namely to dissolve myself in the Organization.

I remember this slogan too: "Only a newborn infant is pure." So who can be pure then? The nursling fumbling for its mother's breast? The little blurry-faced boy beside her looking at the camera? Or the young man entering the banquet hall? That smiling young man was walking toward us. His nom de guerre was Duch. We were all impure, and we would pay.

THE "COMRADE INTERROGATORS" in S-21 were divided into teams. They all tortured people. As for the drivers and guards it's been established that all of them recorded confessions, transported prisoners to Choeung Ek, and there executed and buried them.

Duch: "Everybody in the elite unit of the 703rd division was a killer—that's why they were in S-21! All of them, the ones that transported the prisoners as well as the ones who were permanently stationed at Choeung Ek. Those boys are just afraid to talk to you, poor guys. Don't be hard on them. I accept the whole responsibility." And he laughs.

During those years the men who worked in S-21 were strictly forbidden to leave the place. They worked from

7:00 a.m. to midnight, without respite, every day. They slept, ate, and received medical care—except in cases of serious illness—on the prison grounds. No family, no friends, no women, no leisure time, no visits, no books, no mail. Nothing but torture and death.

From time to time, Duch would call them together for lessons on his methods and the Angkar's dialectics. The men carried out self-criticism in front of their comrades; each self-criticism was recorded and submitted to Duch. Because of this constant monitoring some of the worst atrocities committed in that center are known to us.

Duch himself tells me that a woman who was a former schoolteacher of his was raped with a piece of wood by one of the torturers under his command—a very serious matter, as far as Duch was concerned, because that particular form of torture was not codified.

I think about this teacher as a young woman with her pupil, a poor and brilliant child. I think about the child, sent away to middle school in Siem Reap and then to the lycée in Phnom Penh. I think about him in later years, teaching mathematics in a middle school in Skoun, then going to prison, joining the guerrillas, and becoming "head of security" in Democratic Kampuchea. I think about his former teacher, who was beaten, electrocuted, and starved for days and weeks. I think about the torturer who violated her vagina with a piece of wood. I think about her husband, imprisoned in S-21 at the same moment, who was forced to eat his own excrement. I think about the woman confessing everything, because that was the rule: she confirmed that she was a member of the KGB, or the CIA, or the Vietnamese secret service; she gave the names of traitors and agents; she denounced her entire "network." Then, because she had betrayed her people and her country, she was executed. She was no longer a woman but a piece of trash.

I think about another poor prisoner whose face was covered with cement during one nocturnal interrogation because he refused to confess. Duch was very displeased; that form of torture wasn't codified.

Duch: "The essential thing was for me to accept the Party line. Arrestees were enemies, not people. Comrades, have no feelings! Interrogate! Torture! By way of irrigating the mental soil of my subordinates in S-21 I put the language of slaughter down on paper. And I often organized training sessions."

DURING THE 1960s, Cambodia experienced a fragile peace. My father's guiding vision of education for all wasn't just a dream, but the gap between the cities and the countryside was immense. That injustice was the ground on which the Khmer Rouge prospered. The truth is that the wisdom of country people—which can be discerned, I think, in some of my films—the artistic dimension of their lives, and their traditional know-how, were treated with contempt. Who

tried to develop the art of working in sculpture or cultivate a taste for poetry or an appreciation for the richness of
the Khmer language and the beauty of local crafts? Who
tried to know and educate those poor people? No one, or
hardly anyone. Some whole regions were neglected. By
the French, during the period of the protectorate, which
was cruel and unjust and lasted ninety years. By the Cambodians themselves, after independence was achieved.
Only the revolutionaries gave a voice to those mistreated
and forgotten peasants.

As often happens in revolutions the Khmer Rouge
leaders were the offspring of rather well-to-do families:
Pol Pot, Khieu Samphan, Ieng Sary, and his wife Ieng
Thirith all lived many years in Paris, where they studied Rousseau and Montesquieu, the Enlightenment and
the French Revolution, some Marx, and certain writings
by Stalin and Mao Zedong. They created focus groups,
traveled in Eastern Europe, and met comrades from every
country, especially Algerians. Some of them joined the
French Communist Party. They all studied their cause
in depth. Then they returned to Cambodia. At the same
time, in Phnom Penh, Duch was reading Marx's *Capital*
and especially Mao's *On New Democracy*, in Khmer and
French.

Still today my father is my compass; he was, in his way,
a freedom fighter. For the son of an illiterate peasant to
speak French in a Khmer Rouge village at the time when
the great crimes had already begun was a political act that

signified, "This language is mine. I acquired it to be a man and to pass it on. So make your revolution. Repeat your slogans endlessly. But you cannot take away from me this awareness and this knowledge. If you want my silence, you must kill me."

WHOM DID DUCH not wish to please? Whom did he not want to carry off into his private, sophisticated hell? One afternoon when I can no longer take his attitude, I ask him, "How could an intellectual like you do such things?"

He shoots back his reply, "That's how it is. What do you want me to do now?"

I say, "You could kill yourself, for example. Haven't you ever thought about it?"

He hesitates for an instant, then says, "Yes, but it's not so easy."

I say, "My father killed himself, you know."

This remark makes Duch angry, and his voice becomes shrill and menacing. "Oh, yes, right! Your father, what a hero!"

I reply mildly, "I don't think so. He acted in accordance with his ideas. He respected himself. You made the revolution for justice, didn't you? Being a hero seems easy to me. You jump on a mine, you die for your cause; everywhere is war. But to be a man, to seek liberty and justice, never to abdicate your conscience—that's the real struggle."

Duch doesn't reply. His large eyes are focused some-where behind me. On the guard, on a wall, on the camera, on the past?

On Pol Pot's work table in the jungle, there are books by Marx, Lenin, and Mao. A notebook. Some pencils. Beside the table, a camp bed, and on it a perfectly folded *krama*. The simplicity and truth of the revolution. I've often contemplated that propaganda image. What did they accomplish with their pure ideas? A pure crime.

I'D LIKE THESE pages to take their place far from the slo-gans of the Khmer Rouge, far from violence. Far from the revolution.

For a long time we were deprived of gentleness and sensitivity. Now that Cambodia has found its way back to a form of liberty, a form of peace, now that its glori-ous youth is sweeping away everything, even history, even memory, I'd like this book to give us back our nobility and our dignity.

AT OUR VERY first meeting Duch gives a precise definition of the "old people": the peasants, the workers, the techni-cians of the revolution. I focus on that last category. That's how Duch sees himself—as a technician. Or a technician of the revolution. A few moments earlier, he affirmed that "the movement had to go forward flexibly, nimbly, so that no obstacle might remain. The life of each cog in the movement—especially one of the 'new people'—was not taken into consideration." On another day, he said, "They didn't think about people's lives. They thought about the interests of the movement."

"Technician of the revolution": this special qualification allowed Duch to escape all strictures of class. A revolutionary, even if he was educated, even if he was a bourgeois, was still one of the "old people." He stood with the peasants and the workers. His revolutionary work transformed him, saved him, and brought him closer to both the former Khmer kingdom and the Communist ideal.

Right away, that qualification shows the falseness—and worse, the reversibility—of the classes defined by the Khmer Rouge. What's a peasant or a worker, what's a doctor or a lawyer or a "feudal landowner," et cetera, if certain intellectuals can exit from their class? If the Angkar can wash away their original impurity? If they can escape reeducation or death? To define people, to label them, is to reduce them to mere classification—or in other words, to one's own desire. Defining people is not a way to work for justice, equality, and freedom, and not a way to prepare a future filled with light; it's a way to organize annihilation.

Then comes the question of technique. For the Angkar the revolution wasn't a thought or an idea but a technique one could acquire through action. The revolution wasn't an aspiration; it was a codified practice. The "technician of the revolution" was also an "instrument of the revolution," and the regime's highest distinction was to be a "pure instrument of the revolution." Duch complains that S-21 never received that title.

WHEN I ARRIVE for my interviews with this "technician," I bring material: photocopies of articles, transcriptions of Khmer Rouge slogans, photographs of victims or important revolutionaries, prisoners' confessions with his annotations. I infinitely admire the documentary work of Claude Lanzmann, which is based on speech and the organization of speech. The genius of his *Shoah* is that it lets the viewer see through words.

But I believe that speech can be awakened, amplified, supported by such documents as have managed to escape destruction. That was the case in S-21, where tens of thousands of pages were abandoned in 1979 when Vietnamese troops routed the Khmer Rouge. Sometimes it's useful to hand a sample of that sort of evidence to a person whom I'm filming. It's a way of telling him, "Watch out. I know more than you think; don't lie to me."

Starting with the first day, therefore, I brought along material to show to Duch: I'd copied fifty of the Angkar's slogans, one on each of fifty pages. I asked him to pick out one. Some were threatening, others enigmatic, and still others poetic but cold. He put on his glasses and looked over the collection. He seemed to hesitate, but then he put his hand on a page and read softly, "'To spare you is no profit. To destroy you is no loss.'" He looked up at the ceiling. "That was an important saying. A very profound saying. It came from the Central Committee." Then he added, "You've forgotten an even more important slogan: 'The blood debt must be repaid with blood.'"

I was surprised. "Why that slogan? Why not one that's more ideological?"

Duch fixed me with his eyes: "Mr. Rithy, the Khmer Rouge were all about elimination. Human rights didn't exist."

OF COURSE YOU can always look away. Take your focus off your subject. Let it move aside, drift, disappear—a simple eye movement is enough. Of course you can choose not to look at a country, choose not to know where it is, sigh at the repeated evocations of an unhappy name. You can even decide that what has taken place is incomprehensible and inhuman. Then you look away. It's a universal freedom. You're free to tell yourself that another image will drive out this one, that words can be replaced or erased. And there, it's done: I no longer see the man being forced to eat his own excrement from a spoon, with his hands, arms, and throat tightly bound, his jaws pulled apart, his tongue crushed. I no longer see the Westerner who was encircled with five tires and burned alive in the middle of the street that ran beside S-21. A guard told me he saw the victim gesticulating desperately before he collapsed. Duch explains, "I don't know what happened. I didn't see anything. Nuon Chea gave the order to burn him. He wanted there to be nothing left of him, not a bone, not a bit of flesh. He didn't tell us to burn him alive." I no longer see the baby dashed against a tree. I no longer see them. I no longer see.

I FIND THE FOLLOWING notes that I wrote around the time when *S21: The Khmer Rouge Killing Machine* was released: "It's up to the filmmaker to discover the proper balance. Memory must remain a reference point. What I'm looking for is comprehension; I want to understand the nature of the crime, not to establish a cult of memory. I want to avert repetition." Farther on: "My documentary work is based on listening. I don't fabricate events. I create situations. Insofar as it's humanly possible, I try to present history that's congruous with everyday life and that each individual person can relate to." And finally: "I've never conceived of a film as a response or as a demonstration. I think of it as a questioning." To those who got out in time, to those who escaped the Khmer Rouge, to those who have forgotten or who do not wish to see, I offer these images: that they may be able to see; that they may see.

ONE MORNING ALL of us, all the adults and children in the village, were ordered to gather in a circle. We sat on the ground, worried and silent. A woman stepped into our midst. She was weeping and trembling. Her son, a younger boy whom I knew well, stood up and addressed her vehemently. I've never forgotten his staring eyes and his metallic voice. He was shouting, "You're an enemy of the people. The mangoes you picked belong to the Angkar. You don't have the right to take them and keep them for yourself. Your attitude is bourgeois and shameful. You've acted treasonously. You must be judged by the community."

The woman listened with lowered head as her nine-year-old son insulted her. I was astounded, and all the more so because I myself had picked some mangoes without considering the risk I was taking . . . If a child denounces his own mother, then anything is possible. Politics prevailed over everything, and what politics! On that winter morning—the weather was practically cool—my eyes were opened to the fact that the times had changed. The woman straightened up, gazed into the distance, and acknowledged her fault, at length. "Yes, I picked some mangoes. I picked them in secret. I wanted to keep them for my son and myself. My attitude was individualistic and bourgeois. I thought only of myself. I made a mistake. I'm ashamed. I forgot the people and acted against them. I must change. I must conduct myself better. I beg the Ang-kar to forgive me. I beg forgiveness from the people." I have no memory of ever seeing her again after that.

The Khmer Rouge personnel scrutinized us to gauge our reactions, but we showed none. Nobody moved; we all remained stiff, silent, and empty-eyed. Fear tightened my throat. A few days later my sisters and I were sent away, scattered to different parts of the region, while my parents remained in the village with my young nephew and niece. The individual had to be dissolved in the organization, in conformity to the slogan: "Renounce all you own, your father, your mother, your family!"

WAS IT THEN, more or less, that a new and unique style of haircut was instituted throughout the country? Or was it earlier, at the same time as the definitive prohibition of col-ored clothing? I remember that long hair, even bound up, had disappeared back in Koh Tauch. Long hair was a femi-nine, and therefore sexual, symbol. Or a sign of negligence. Or of a desire to be different. All the Khmer Rouge person-nel took Pol Pot as their model and wore their hair cleanly cut behind the ears. For the girls, there was the "omega" cut, as my sisters secretly called it: bangs in the front and gathered in the back. But note that shaving your head was also sternly frowned upon, because it recalled the Buddhist monks. Child that I was, I learned this fact only later.

Once again I ask myself: What kind of a political regime exerts an influence that extends from the bedroom to the cooperative? What kind of regime abolishes school, family, justice, the entirety of the previous social organization; rewrites history; believes neither in knowledge nor in science; displaces the population; puts constraints on human relationships, both friendly and romantic; governs every profession; invents some words and forbids others? What sort of regime considers the absence of people preferable to imperfect people—imperfect, that is, according to the regime's criteria? Was it Marxism, regarded as a science? An ideocracy, in the sense that abstract ideas triumphed over all? "Polpotism," wrought with violence and purity?

The answer perhaps lies in Democratic Kampuchea's coat of arms: a railroad track crosses rice fields as symmetrical as blocks of cement. On the horizon, a factory with pitched roofs and smoking chimneys. No escape possible. The rails aren't actually rails, even though it's impossible to look at them and not think about rails. They're low walls leading to a levee, and an irrigation canal runs down the center from the factory to a dam. Democratic Kampuchea was all about irrigation and factories, peasants and workers.

Of course this was an emblem of struggle, a grim, deliberate signal in the tradition of Soviet posters. Everything starts with work, and nothing worthwhile can be attained except through work. No living creature is portrayed. No face. No joy. Even the stalks of wheat that frame the image like a menacing laurel wreath are disturbing.

I'm struck by an obvious fact. The straight lines don't say, *We dream of reaching that horizon. It's our big evening.* Instead, they say, *There's only one track, and there's only one destination: an industrial building belching smoke.* How can one look at this emblem and not think of imprisonment and destruction? For me this is the message of the coat of arms: *There will have to be much weeding, planting, replanting, soaking, drying, fighting, forging, and manufacturing, and many men will have to melt away before this world can come.*

I REMEMBER THE DAY when a Party leader asked me my name. "Rithy," I was told, must be discarded as a bourgeois given name. At thirteen I became "Comrade Thy." One year later a bad infestation of lice caused me to shave my head. After that, I was called "Comrade Bald." Then I sustained a serious foot injury. Since I walked with difficulty I became "Comrade Tractor." During a period when my behavior was irritating the Khmer Rouge, they told me, "You walk like a councillor's son." (They used the French word for "councillor"—*conseil*—which they took to mean "minister"; in other words I had an arrogant way of walking.) And that became my name: "Councillor's Son."

I understand that the revolutionaries, when they first went underground, had to change their names, and that this practice became a custom. But to reduce the other to a gesture, to a mechanism, to a part of his body is not a way to spread the revolution. It's a way of dehumanizing people, of holding them in your clenched fist.

Until the liberation I remained "Comrade Bald," and a good thing too; it meant I no longer bore my father's name, which was too well known. I had no family. I had no name. I had no face. And so, because I was nothing anymore, I was still alive.

"ON THE AFFECTIONS," the sixth fragment of the French revolutionary Louis Antoine de Saint-Just's *Fragments concerning Republican Institutions*, contains the following prescriptions:

> Every man twenty-one years of age and older is required to declare in the temple who his friends are. This declaration must be renewed every year during the month of Ventôse.
>
> If a man gives up a friend, he is required upon summons to state his reasons for having done so before the people in the temple. If he refuses, he shall be banished.
>
> Friends may not make written contracts or litigate against one another.
>
> In battle, friends are to be positioned near one another.
>
> Those who have remained friends all their lives are to be buried in the same tomb.

Friends shall wear mourning for one another. The people shall elect the tutors of surviving children from among their father's friends.

If a man commits a crime, his friends shall be banished.

Friends shall dig a deceased friend's grave and prepare his funeral services. They and the children of the deceased shall scatter flowers on his burial place.

He who says that he does not believe in friendship, or who has no friends, shall be banished.

A man convicted of ingratitude shall be banished.

I reread this discourse, in which there are many orders and little friendship. "He . . . who has no friends shall be banished." Which political regime is the most inhuman? The one that prescribes human welfare. In such a case there are no citizens anymore. And no thinking beings.

In the Angkar's view there were no individuals. We were elements. Mathematical units. Neutral matter, gathered for practical reasons into groups of five or ten: boys and girls, young or less young. We were never alone. And we were banished.

I GOT SENT to the "front," that is, to a worksite five hours' walk from the village where my parents were. We were all between ten and fourteen years old, including the unit leaders. Only the "schoolmistresses"—who taught us ideology—were eighteen. Everything we had we had in common. Everything. Before, we'd boil water from the rice fields before drinking it. I'd learned to make fire by rubbing the shards of broken plates against metal. The sparks would ignite kapok fibers laid in a bamboo stalk.

But a Khmer Rouge soldier came up to me and said, "Why are you making a fire? It's forbidden to make fires! Fire is reserved to the cooperative!" We were subjected to a series of searches, and all our possessions were confiscated, including our cans and buckets. Nothing belonged to us anymore. I therefore followed my comrades' example: I mustered all my courage and drank water from the pools and the fields.

I was immediately assigned to a dike-building project. There were hundreds of us, armed with shovels, palanquins, and bamboo stretchers. Together we formed an exhausted waterwheel, barely turning under the tropical sun. It seemed that no earth-moving equipment of any kind was available. The message was clear: *We revolutionaries have come this far by the strength of our own arms; we can do better than any machine.*

I know a repetitive and fascinating propaganda film. It starts with a Peugeot 404 that's being turned into a paddle-wheel mill. Two "technicians of the revolution" bustle around the vehicle, smiling at the camera. Look at what we're doing with these engines, with this sheet metal, with this civilization. Look at what we do with impure pieces of machinery: they are assigned to the group. From now on they will participate in the irrigation of our fields. In this new usage the cars—the Peugeot 404s—were "new people." They too got reeducated.

Starting at dawn I dug. I shored up. We didn't speak. The task seemed immense. I worked in the fields too, bending down to the earth from the height of my thirteen years. Not thinking about anything. Listening to the anthems blaring out from the loudspeakers. One evening I had a fleeting vision of my paternal grandfather: I was pulling weeds, just as he was. I was a child of the Kingdom of Angkor.

THE ARCHIVES ARE alive. Nothing in them is silent. A photograph. A sheet of paper marked with red ink. I think about the woman who refused to be photographed from the front when she entered S-21. She was a professor. She faced away, holding herself obliquely to the camera, and almost smiled. In one of her handwritten confessions, she evoked Cuba, which was also on the revolutionary road, but where the revolutionaries "aren't killing everybody or starving the people." Thirty years later her massage reaches us. It's often combative. Sometimes despairing, but not always. We should listen for those words, listen to that murmur, and we should recall Taing Siv Leang—I write her name—so that she may remain among us, she and her smile.

AT NIGHTFALL, WE left the rice fields. After a brief meal, we got back to our hammocks. These were tightly bound, one above the other, to a pair of large palms: a total of eight or nine hammocks in all, rising like the rungs of a ladder between the two trees. This arrangement was supposed to deter snakes, giant ants, scorpions, and spiders. The webs of black cord were our refuges. They protected us from the night, with its rustling and its cries. Our hammocks cradled us. When his turn came, one of us would poke the fire at the foot of one of the giant trees, so that we could stay dry in spite of the dew—we had but one article of clothing.

I would put myself in a hammock in the middle, and in keeping with Khmer tradition I'd make up a ghost story. The boys in my group often asked me for one.

I remember a yarn that I'm going to summarize here in a few lines, but which, with the help of many details, I used to stretch out over the course of an entire evening. The night, chattering and restless, was going to win in the end, but we still had words.

A traveler passes by an abandoned village. In the distance he can hear the howling of wolves. He walks past one house, then another. Nobody home. Everybody except the traveler knows that this village is haunted. A delicious aroma of spiced soup is wafting around the third house the traveler approaches. A prettily dressed woman greets him and asks him where he's headed. The traveler tells her the truth. She disappears for a few moments and then comes back. The two of them sit on a mat, talk, and learn a bit about each other, and the traveler has some of the excellent soup. He forgets the wolves howling around the abandoned village. The woman leans toward him with shining eyes. But at the moment when she's about to serve him again, her ladle falls between two floorboards and down to the ground under the house. She opens her pretty mouth and sticks out her tongue, which extends farther and farther, slips between the floorboards, stretches down to the ground, and retrieves the ladle . . . a sorceress! The traveler leaps abruptly to his feet, but too late: the woman smiles at him and kills him.

Thanks to my talents as a storyteller I was assigned to the cooperative's kitchens and thus able to leave the dike and the rice fields behind. I was saved from death by exhaustion. I prepared the soup in my turn. I boiled rice. I accepted delivery of the day's catch, fine-looking fish reserved for the "schoolmistresses." When you work in the kitchen, your nutrition level is bound to improve. You can scrape out the bottom of the pots, where everything's greasy and cooked and hard, and it strengthens your resistance. Besides the cook serves the leaders; he knows who eats what. Strategic information.

I cooked for children, which meant that my first priority was to serve the children of the Khmer Rouge, just as the cook for adults served the Khmer Rouge first. Most of the time, they would eat apart from the rest of us. Communism or not, equality has its limits.

I continued to tell ghost stories in the evenings. Because of my storytelling and my cooking, the group leader would occasionally give me an authorization that allowed me to visit my parents.

I'D LEAVE AT DAWN, walking alone on a deserted trail that skirted some yellowing rice fields. There were no trees. I passed only two waterholes. I hurried along, almost running, because the sandy path burned my feet so much. It was like flaming powder. After a journey of five to six hours, I'd arrive.

My parents had been relocated. They were now in Trum, twelve or fifteen miles from the preceding village, but situated like it on an arid plain. There my mother had built a cabin. She'd found some branches and skillfully trimmed them, assembled boards one by one, and arranged layers of palm leaves, tamping them down to make a solid roof. The structure included a small, separate room that served as the kitchen.

I'd spend the night with them. My visits were brief, but I was always so happy to see them again.

I discovered that my mother had succeeded in keeping her little ax: an essential tool. She'd convinced the head of the village that she absolutely needed that ax.

She'd leave regularly to fetch water—four hours there, four hours back, traveling on foot and carrying a plastic jerrican. As for my father, he was exhausted. He hardly walked at all anymore. When he did, he'd wander about in his black undershirt, a legacy from former times. Like all the elegant men of a certain generation, he used to wear a white undershirt under a dress shirt. One of those articles, dyed black, became his last outfit. At dawn when I'd leave, he'd smile at me sadly with my mother at his side.

I run to the trail, which starts at the edge of the village. The morning fog is already lifting. I turn around one more time. I look at them but make no sign.

IN THE SPRING, to make a change from ghosts and apparitions, I told our group the story of the fabulous expedition to the moon. In fact, I recounted the entire Apollo mission, including the famous words spoken by Armstrong, whose first name I didn't know: "That's one small step for a man, one giant leap for mankind." Many of my comrades didn't believe me and said, "That's not true, you made it up. It's impossible!" They were all the more reluctant to credit the story because the Khmer people have many festivals, traditions, oracles, and legends connected with the moon. When I was a child I would ask my parents about the craters on the moon, and they'd tell me, "Rithy, those aren't craters.

They're the faces of an old man and an old woman who live up there, under a tree . . ." I'd stare at the cold star and dream. That image has never left my mind.

On the evening when my comrades said I was making up the moon story, I replied that I hadn't invented a thing, and that I'd seen an astronaut on television, climbing down from his lunar lander, the famous LEM. The image quivered. Everything went slowly. I described the first steps in the black dust. I talked about the astronauts' experiments, about Armstrong gathering samples with a shovel. And I concluded with the return of the three men to Earth. Someone asked, "But who are those people?" I replied, "They're Americans." What a mistake! There was a long, pained silence, and then we went to sleep.

The following evening the "schoolmistress" for the groups of young people summoned me in a tone that admitted no appeal: "Comrade Thy! Approach!" I stepped into the center of the circle, and she fixed me with a fierce stare before she spoke again: "Comrade! You must do a self-criticism. Yesterday you regaled your comrades with stories about men landing on the moon, and you sang the praises of the American imperialists. Such tales are inventions. Lies. Your conduct is unacceptable. When you spread those fables, you betray the revolution. You betray your comrades. We'll hear what you have to say."

Her cabin was pretty close to ours, and she'd no doubt heard my story herself, or else someone reported it to her. Obviously I hadn't thought about getting in trouble. The Apollo 11 project amazed and fascinated me so much that I'd let my guard down. I was far from feeling any hatred for America and capitalism. Before I spoke I had to listen to the self-criticisms of the seven or eight boys who'd been listening to me the previous evening. They too were guilty: they had listened to me without a qualm, and moreover they'd probably believed me in the end. They stood up and explained that they'd been wrong, that they'd fallen into a trap, that they shouldn't have paid any attention to my stories, that they'd be more vigilant from now on, that the Angkar surely guided their lives.

When my turn came I gravely repeated what had been said without understanding a lot of it: America, imperialism, propaganda, lies, the moon. I was stared at coldly. I silently exhorted myself not to cry, not to tremble. To remain calm. To do nothing to aggravate my case. My self-criticism was total, for in the world of the Khmer Rouge, time didn't exist. And so I went back and criticized my ghost stories too for not being sufficiently revolutionary. After an hour, I was exhausted. Humiliated. Sad and defeated. The storyteller was dead. And I wasn't a cook anymore either.

The following day I marched with my comrades to the rice fields, where the white sun of the revolution was already beginning to bite.

HIM HUY, A guard recently assigned to S-21, writes his self-criticism:

> I helped my parents. My family. I always speak properly to people, even old people.
>
> My weak points: I sometimes use incorrect words. I'm quick to anger. I like amusement. I like going out to the theater and watching movies. Dancing. Listening to the radio. Sometimes I've stolen pieces of fruit, but I did it so I could eat them.
>
> My romantic life: I was in love with a girl. But I didn't touch her body. And I didn't use improper words. I loved her in secret.
>
> I know the character I've developed during the revolution. I apply myself to carrying out the missions that the Communist Party has entrusted me with. I don't hesitate. I don't protest any mission, even if it's difficult and I have to suffer to carry it out. I fight to complete it.
>
> Weak points: I sometimes use incorrect words in front of my comrades. I joke too much. When I'm in command, I get angry very fast. In monitoring the rank and file, I'm not regular enough or sufficiently serious about enemy activity. I take enemy activity too lightly. I'm not strict enough in my work. Not intelligent enough or rapid enough in performing my mission. I haven't learned enough from experience or applied what I've learned often enough. I'm still too careless. My superiors have had to summon me to regain my position.

What I must change: I vow to correct my character, which isn't properly revolutionary. I will correct it with all my heart. I will apply myself to recovering a revolutionary position, according to the principles of the proletarian class and the Communist Party.

UPON THE ARRIVAL of the Khmer Rouge, people seemed to have been hypnotized. This happened initially because they believed—as my father did, in his fashion—that the revolutionaries were right. From the exterminator's good faith to the exterminee's eyes. It's a question not just of belief but of rational belief.

Today, I know that speed was a decisive factor—even though it seems in retrospect not to have been so important. We didn't have the time to be fascinated or convinced. We were immediately displaced. Starved. Separated. Terrorized. Deprived of speech and of all our rights. We were broken. Submerged in hunger and fear. And in six months, my whole family disappeared.

I was thirteen years old, standing upright in a cattle car. Sometimes the door was partly open, but I didn't jump.

The passion for confession is fearful. It can make you doubt the truth. Worse: it can make you doubt the importance of the truth.

On the evening when I performed my self-criticism, the evening after I told the story of the Apollo 11 mission,

I didn't think for a moment about explaining myself. Or defending myself. I said *what it was necessary for me to say*. I conformed myself to the desires of the Khmer Rouge leaders. I spoke in order to be able to return to silence. To be invisible is to be a living being; almost an individual.

Duch mentions the principle that stands above all others: the primacy of "proletarian truth." Later he attributes its formulation to his superior, Nuon Chea: "We must think about proletarian truth. And we must not think about bourgeois truth."

OFTEN, DURING THE filming of *S21: The Khmer Rouge Killing Machine*, I ask the "comrade guards" to "make the gestures" of the period for my camera. I specify that I'm not asking them to "act," but to "make the gestures"—a way of extending their words. If necessary they start, stop, and start again ten or twenty times. Their reflexes return; I see what really happened. Or what's impossible. The method and the truth of the extermination appear.

In S-21 the Angkar's discipline is absolute: the prisoner admits that he's betrayed the revolution; he signs one or more detailed confessions; these latter are consigned to the people in the person of Duch, who reports directly to Pol Pot's Standing Committee. Once this security work is completed, justice can be done. His eyes blindfolded, the culprit is taken to Choeung Ek and executed there. Buried. Erased forever.

In S-21 Duch demands a confession: a new history that erases history. The confession may be incoherent or absurd; it makes no difference. The person who recounts and constructs the new history is a traitor. He speaks as a traitor. He acknowledges his crimes and his lies. He's condemned by the account he's required to give.

Sometimes Duch himself gets to work. He rewrites certain confessions, for example that of Nget You, known as Hong. Duch strikes out entire pages that don't suit him and adapts the forced confessions to his own needs or logic before having them typed.

When you analyze this process meticulously, when you "make the gestures," you see how much Duch has lied and continues to lie. How slippery his words are. For example, I show him a photograph taken during his tenure by one of the photographers in S-21. Bloodstains are perfectly visible on the floor and the wall. Duch answers that he never saw any blood in any of the buildings.

Then I give him a photograph of Bophana. At first, he doesn't recognize her. Doesn't remember. However, under this face there's a note in his hand, dated September 26, 1976: "This tart is the wife of the contemptible Deth and a daughter of the contemptible Ly Thean Chek." Now Bophana's father was Hourt Cheng, a respected personage in Baray district and even throughout the whole of Kampong

Thom province, where Duch and Mam Nay were teachers. Bophana wrote her father's name in her confession. But Duch, with his crude fabrication, made this young woman the daughter of an enemy deputy and therefore an enemy herself.

I press him, "Bophana wrote love letters; in his responses Deth quoted Shakespeare. You seized those letters and used them as proof of her treason. Don't you remember?"

Duch: "Did I make any notes in Bophana's file?"

Me: "Yes. Look, all the writing in red is yours. You certainly read those letters . . ."

He examines the confession. "Yes, that's my handwriting . . ." He sighs. His left hand picks up a new page.

DUCH HESITATES. His fingers brush that photographed face. He asks for more time. I insist. After further prompting recollection returns, and Duch eventually reconstructs the young woman's entire story, from her arrest to the death of her husband. As he'd done with all the confessions obtained in S-21 Duch had read, annotated, and questioned her successive versions. In the record books he hadn't been able to burn in time in January 1979, he'd written "to be destroyed" opposite her name.

For four years the capital remained entirely deserted, except for the government, a few embassies, and S-21.

Duch admits that *"Everyone saw, heard, and knew.* Even with your eyes shut, it was obvious that there were no people in Phnom Penh anymore." (The emphasis is mine.)

I regret that the tribunal didn't organize some in-depth confrontations on these matters, if only to establish a historical documentation. Why was Nuon Chea—who was Duch's superior in the hierarchy after Son Sen, now dead—never called to testify in Duch's trial, even though he was awaiting his own trial in the same prison? There are hundreds of confessions that bear the following annotation, handwritten by Duch: "to be submitted to Comrade Nuon Chea." Some other confessions are "to be submitted to Comrade Van," that is, Ieng Sary, Democratic Kampuchea's foreign minister from 1975 to 1979 and currently in prison. While Duch was being tried, Nuon Chea and Ieng Sary were in their cells, not a hundred feet from the court.

Similarly certain registers should have been examined; every column, every line, every signature, every comment deserves an analysis, a discussion, some confrontations. That's the way to make everything come spilling out.

The trial of John Demjanjuk, accused of complicity in the murder of 28,060 Jews in the Sobibor prison camp, took place in Munich from 2009 to 2011. According to the Paris newspaper *Le Monde*, the proceedings permitted the examination of close to 40,000 documents, "of which more than a hundred were patiently read aloud, day after day, by the judges in front of a rather sparse audience. . . . Thus ten sessions or so were required to authenticate the 'Trawiki

ID card,' the public prosecutor's main piece of evidence. It took many more sessions to evoke Sobibor, which was, as has often been repeated, 'a camp whose only residents were the people who were going to die during the day and the people who participated in putting them to death.'"

His eyes turned heavenward, Duch murmurs, "An immense prison—I actually saw the place! But I didn't want to know or see the sufferings of those who were there. I left. I saw the buildings, but I didn't want to see the suffering. My feelings prevented me from seeing it. Even if I saw it, I didn't pay attention."

Later he says, "I didn't help anyone. Who would die, and where and when? I left that to karma, and let the devil take the hindmost!"

He concludes by declaring, "With the passage of time, one forgets these unimportant details. Certain things went beyond what would have been acceptable. However I did them. And so I force myself to forget so that I won't be too tormented. That's how I do it: I try hard to forget, and by dint of trying, I really do forget."

WE WERE DIGGING an irrigation canal when I received a blow from a pickax on the inside of my foot. The metal cut into the bone. Not a serious wound, but extremely painful. For a few days afterward I limped around. Then, what with the damp earth, the dust, the perspiration, the mud, the stagnant water, and the lack of food and sleep, my cut got infected. It grew red and swollen; the open gash made me suffer a little more every day. The flesh decayed and fell off like strips of wet paper. I was rotten, and my own smell—like old sugar—nauseated me. The Khmer Rouge in charge summoned me and said, "The Angkar is sending you back to live with your parents. Have your injury looked after and then come back!" This show of understanding terrified me. Since when were humans looked after? Since when were the living looked after?

I was carried in a cart to our cabin in Trum, where my mother tried everything in her power to heal my wound, including poultices and tamarind leaves, but the situation was incredible: no medical supplies were available anymore, no disinfectant, no bandages, no sticking plaster, no antiseptic. I can still see my mother, searching desperately for a clean cloth to protect my skin. Everything was dirty. Everything was old. She left with a bucket to fetch water from a source several miles away. Then she spent hours washing and rinsing the yellowed strips of material she used to wrap my wound.

I was bedridden. If I moved about the cabin, I did so on my hands. There was almost nothing in there; our whole lives were reduced to some boards, some lianas, and a couple of bundles my family had been hauling around since we left Phnom Penh.

It was around that time when my father began to say to anyone who'd listen, "I'm not eating anything that doesn't resemble food fit for human beings." As he spoke, he knew he'd try to refrain from eating at all. It wasn't a political gesture; it was his life itself, his will to defend his idea of dignity and progress to the end. As if he wanted to be the last man.

My father had traveled a lot: to Egypt, to France, to the United States, and to various countries in Eastern Europe. Yugoslavia particularly interested him—I remember that we received some magazines from Belgrade every month in the mail. He had understood that the new power would be implacable, and that the process of dehumanization wouldn't stop; that ideology would carry all before it.

MY MOTHER SEARCHED everywhere for rice for him. When she procured some he'd eat a spoonful and give us the rest. My little nephew and niece, five and seven years old, even went to steal some rice from the village granary, otherwise known as the village boss's house. They scraped the floorboards and gathered up a bit of unhulled rice in their childish hands. They were caught in the act and arrested. My mother got furious: "If you don't want them to steal rice, all you have to do is give us some!" Nobody knew how to react to such audacity, and she took the children home.

Little by little, my father stopped feeding himself. He'd decided that it was all over. He grew very thin and hardly walked anymore.

He'd sit in the shade and doze. Sometimes he'd open his stricken eyes and look at me queerly, with what I think was a little pity. Death knows.

I was afraid. Our common room wasn't very big, but I still managed to put some distance between my waning father and me. I stayed on the threshold of the cabin door. Or I jammed my mat against the wall and closed my eyes. I didn't want to see his decline. I was angry at him, and I felt like shouting, "We've got some rice! So eat! Get your strength up!" But what could I do? Nothing. And to whom could I talk? Nobody.

My mother took care of him, but she was extremely worried. One morning she came looking for me in the kitchen, where I was tending a pan of rice. "Rithy," she said, "your father's about to leave. Come."

I slipped to his side and knelt on the creaking floorboards. My father lay stretched out on a mat, his eyes closed, his cheeks hollow, his skin gray. He was barely breathing. We waited in silence. And then I saw his end. Yes, I saw his breath stop. The rise and fall of his lungs ceased. I photographed that moment in my memory. It was unthinkable. I didn't understand why my father had acted as he had, why he'd gone away, why he'd left us alone with the Khmer Rouge, alone in that terrifying world. Today I blame myself for not having really been at his side, for not having been able to share his silence.

The burial had to take place quickly, before nightfall, because of the heat. My mother had saved one good white sheet; she unfolded it without a word. I touched the embroidery. It was unreal, like touching the past, the old days. The body was quickly wrapped in that shroud, and then in a thin metal sheet.

My mother refused to attend the funeral, which she found unworthy of her husband and his convictions, unworthy of his family. She refused the zinc and the water-logged earth of the rice fields. And so it was that my big sister accompanied our father's body. There were rumors that the dead were being disinterred and despoiled. Sometimes eaten. Would the shroud be stolen? We never tried to find out.

That night I stayed with my mother. It was the rainy season. Heat seemed to rise from the earth like a kind of invisible water. We sat on a mat, leaning against a partition made of palm leaves. Slowly, her voice low, my mother described to me my father's funeral the way she imagined it, the way it should have been, traditional and respectful. "You see there, walking in the first row behind the wooden coffin, the representatives of the students; following them, the teachers; then the representatives of the ministry, carrying wreaths of flowers; and then the family. We're all gathered together there. Brothers, sisters, cousins, aunts. Nephews and nieces.

We've come from all over the country. Some have arrived after walking for two days. Others have come by train or bus. We're at his side. Silent. Full of love."

She knew my father had ended his days with dignity, which was what he'd wished to do. That night she swept me away into a Khmer legend. She didn't miss any stage of the funeral ceremony. We called upon our family's ancestors, and then we fell silent.

Our funeral-in-words lasted the whole night. We drifted in the frail vessel my mother conjured up, and while we did, my father's passing seemed less painful. But when the dawn came, we were alone.

My mother wept very little, which surprised me; she'd always been very close to her husband, the father of her nine children. When she did weep she wept in silence. It was almost invisible. Later I realized that she just didn't want to give in. To weep was to give in. We had to face the Khmer Rouge proudly and show them that we were worthy and upright, that we thought as my father had thought. That we were above drama. That we were human beings.

In the end my mother told us, "You must eat your father's rice. You need it." She didn't take any, but each of the rest of us had a small portion. Many years later I still remember the taste of that spoonful of rice, strange and bitter, as if I had stolen it.

I BELIEVE MY FAITH in the cinema comes from that day. I believe in the image, even if it's staged, interpreted, worked on. In spite of dictatorship one can film a true image.

ON CERTAIN NIGHTS I bend down to the earth. My knees sink into it. I cup my childish hands. I suck in the brown water through my lips; it smells like old, wet straw. You who believe in a better world, a world without classes, without currency, a radiant world that wishes everyone well, have you tasted the rice field gurgling in your throat? Do you know the savor of pools where eels have slept? I awaken with a start.

DUCH IS CLASSIFYING his files. He lines up folders and pages, piling them on the table with somewhat jerky movements. Then he rises to his feet and says, "I'm going to reflect upon the crimes committed against my people. And on what makes me suffer the most."

WITHOUT RICE, WITHOUT WATER, without strength, how to resist? Without friends, without brothers and sisters in arms, how to escape? How to remain human? One had to survive. That was our first duty. Our first battle. To rebel was first of all to live. Or rather: to stay alive.

AFTER HIS WIFE'S DEATH a father is left to raise his five-year-old daughter alone. While plowing one early morning he finds two snails in the rich earth. He proudly shows them to his daughter, who's sitting on higher ground nearby. In the midst of famine, two snails are a treasure. At the moment when he's slipping them into his pocket, some Khmer Rouge approach. They call him an individualist. An enemy of the Angkar. They beat him and tie him to a post on the edge of the rice field. The hours pass. The temperature becomes unbearable. The man groans. Ants crawl up his body, at first hundreds of ants, then thousands. They invade his mouth, his throat, his ears, his eyes. The man writhes, shouts until he can shout no more, collapses. Then a peasant woman comes up, takes the little girl's hand—she's remained there since the early morning—and says, "Come with me." They walk to the village together. Years later that child weeps silently in front of my camera.

As I write these lines, I feel stiffness take over my hand, skip past my wrist, and run up my elbow to my shoulder. Like being grazed by a needle.

KHMER PROVERB: "Truth is a poison."

"THE LANGUAGE OF SLAUGHTER." That's the expression Duch uses in his prison. I look at the photograph from S-21 that shows a sorrowful-looking mother standing up with an infant in her arms. The mother will be tortured. Both of them will die, but separately. In another photograph a nearly naked child is stretched out on the ground in a wooden cell two feet wide, on S-21's first floor. That child's going to die too.

In general, the children of enemies—called, in fact, "child-enemies"—were dashed against tree trunks. But at least one case is known of a baby thrown out of a third-floor window before the eyes of its parents. The guard who gave this testimony buried the child at the request of his boss.

The Khmer Rouge devise the word *kamtech*, which I ask Duch to define—he's written it thousands of times and uses it to this day. Duch is clear: *kamtech* means to destroy and then to erase all trace: to *reduce to dust*. The tribunal translates it as "to crush," which is obviously quite different. The language of slaughter is in that word. Let nothing remain, no trace of life, no trace of death. Let the death itself be erased.

That's the secret that explains why the terror could go on for so long and never face a revolt. Thus Bophana's clothes and other belongings—"spoils of war"—were given away to all comers as soon as she was transferred to S-21. Bophana disappeared; everything pertaining to Bophana disappeared. And such an erasure is an ungraspable death.

Duch gives details: when a prisoner died, his or her family was not notified; the body was not released; and no explanation was given. The Angkar had no need to justify itself—because the Angkar was the only family.

I'VE WRITTEN ABOUT my father that "he knew communism." I take responsibility for the accuracy of those words, even if some people think that true communism wasn't really tried, and that the idea of communism abides. Words dart and flutter about. So maybe there's no human history, no reality, but rather reasoning and hypotheses and the chamber of ideas—which is a heaven.

So many years, so many countries were apparently not enough. So many millions of victims. Each person assumes his responsibilities; when you choose certain words, you choose your weapon. However, as I've written, we didn't flee the country in 1975. Once the upheavals inherent in every revolution had passed, my father thought, he'd be a useful man. He'd work for the education of every citizen, he imagined, and thus for equality and justice.

But from the first moments of its existence, the regime acted with cruelty. Death was everywhere. What my father had seen in Eastern Europe—the lack of freedom, the omnipotence of the group, the passion for secrecy, the general poverty, the desire to escape—was coming to pass in Democratic Kampuchea at breakneck speed. And the speed of the transition to ideal communism was directly proportional to the number of dead.

One day Duch informs me, "It's a mistake to look at the Great Leap Forward from the standpoint of economic development. The Great Leap Forward was the destruction of social classes." Pol Pot wanted there to be only two classes, and very quickly.

Of course it's impossible to compare the Soviet, Chinese, and Cambodian regimes. But I see in all of them the camps and the prisons, the violence, the paranoia. I see everywhere the hatred of men and ideas. To the intellectuals of the West who have composed odes and poems, created *dazibao* (big-character posters), written tracts and enthusiastic articles and books; who still today, after so much progress toward democracy, aspire to a new, purified communism; and who hold forth in chic salons, smoothing the velvet of their radicalism, I say: there is only one man.

I COPY AND RECOPY two phrases. I try to imagine, calmly, simply, what each word signifies. They're human phrases. They refer to actions perpetrated by humans. Upon other humans. But there's no more humanity.

To dissect a living woman.
To take all a woman's blood.

I copy them again. What cries does a human being utter when her belly is split open? When her liver is cut out? When her organs are removed? What cries does a human being utter when she realizes that all her blood is being taken and she'll never get up again? These experiments were performed in S-21. Duch explains, "The vivisection was done to study anatomy. But I was against the idea." Yet we know it was carried out.

I don't want anyone telling me I'm a voyeur. I work with facts. Images. Archives. I work with history, even if it makes us uncomfortable. I verify everything. I translate every word. I analyze every sign—what's said, what's written, what's hidden. If I have a doubt, I cut. And I show what was.

PRIMO LEVI FEARED he wouldn't be believed. My fear: that the story I'm going to tell may cause suffering to people close to me. So I move aside. I dream that the words fade away.

Duch: "Of course I see, but my unconscious prevents me from seeing."

LOUIS ALTHUSSER, in a letter to his wife dated September 12, 1969: "The end of the exploitation of man by man will be the end of the exploitation of one unconscious entity by another."

⎯⎯

VANN NATH: "Duch sat in an armchair and watched me paint Pol Pot's portrait. Sometimes I felt him very close to me; he'd be scrutinizing the portrait over my shoulder. He used to talk to me about famous painters like van Gogh and Picasso. When I painted Pol Pot's hair I avoided making any sudden movements so that Duch wouldn't be able to observe any disrespect. . . . I worked on the head gently, with light touches. And as for the surface of the face, I thought it would be best to give it a pink color and smooth, delicate skin as beautiful as a young virgin's. And so Duch was content and accepted the picture."

⎯⎯

IN HIS CELL, Duch incessantly draws mounds of skulls. He even goes so far as to offer me one of his sketches, an extraordinarily somber and muddled work: as before, skulls, skulls by the hundreds; and in the center Pol Pot.

At Duch's request I bring him a Bible. And, from Paris, a French grammar book and some HB pencils. He loves to converse with me in French and proudly recites passages from Balzac or poems.

Sometimes we talk about painting. He knows but doesn't care for the work of Vincent van Gogh. However, he seems to be fascinated by the self-portraits the artist made after slicing off his ear. Is it the difficulty of picturing oneself? Of capturing one's own face in its entirety—or rather in its integrity, if I dare put it that way? Is it the impossibility of showing *a man's head* to people and society?

He criticizes my friend Nath: "He isn't a great painter; there isn't anything true to life in his pictures." I reply that Nath's work deals powerfully with memory, and that's what one must analyze. Nath is a painter *and* a survivor—and a survivor *because* he was a painter. You can't understand his work except through that perspective. Now Duch, discoursing to me upon aesthetics and pictorial technique, seems to have forgotten that Nath painted portraits of Pol Pot for a year in the very heart of S-21—and that he worked exclusively from photographs and propaganda films. Duch concludes, bizarrely, by saying, "Don't repeat what I told you to Nath. I'm just talking, you know . . ."

He doesn't like Picasso, particularly his "bull's heads." Is it the affirmation of desire and power that bothers Duch? Is it the painter reveling in his freedom? I think the only artist he sincerely and lastingly admires is Leonardo da Vinci. He mentions the *Mona Lisa* and explains to me that she looks like a Khmer woman. He murmurs, "There's something Cambodian in that portrait." Does he see in her an heiress of the Kingdom of Angkor, I wonder? Is it her placid beauty that touches him? The purity of her clothes, her hands, her bosom? Or is it the work of the Renaissance that attracts him, so balanced, so—let's dare to say it—mathematical?

I hereby offer a hypothesis: Duch is fascinated by those eyes that stare at us yet look past us, by those eyes that can't be caught and held. As if the rest of the sitter were just an envelope of flesh. As if there were no living being.

I WALKED BAREFOOT for four years. It seems to me I've never lost the rough brown calluses. Or maybe my skin has regained its human aspect and it's my heart that's hardened.

DURING THE FIRST WEEKS we were worried about the disappearances. We knew nothing about the country, about our families, about our friends, about our neighbors; about ourselves. All of a sudden, one person or another was no longer there, and it was as if they'd never been there. Erasure. Everything was done to break human relationships. The transfers from one place to another were incessant and illogical. The Khmer Rouge would show up late one evening and proclaim: "By order of the Angkar: You must leave. Immediately." No appeal was possible. Everyone picked up his bag. Sometimes we set out at night. Destination unknown. We were objects.

I'm repeating myself, but repetition is indispensable when the subject of your investigation is a great crime: I doubt whether such a regime, where the whole of life was controlled to such a degree, had ever existed before. What can be said about a country that becomes per se one enormous work camp? How can we qualify those 1.7 million deaths in four years, a total reached without the means of mass extermination? A dictatorship by terror? A crime against humanity? The suicide of a nation?

Behind those crimes there were a small handful of intellectuals, a powerful ideology, a rigorous organization, an obsession with control and therefore with secrecy, total contempt for the individual, and the status of death as an absolute recourse. Yes, there was a human project.

This is the reason why I dislike the expressions "suicide of a nation" and "autogenocide" and "politicide" so profoundly, no matter that they suit everyone's convenience. A nation that commits suicide is a unique body, a body cut off from the greater body of nations. Such a nation is enigmatic, impenetrable. It's a sick nation, maybe even an insane one. And the world remains innocent. The crimes committed by Democratic Kampuchea, and the intention behind those crimes, were incontrovertibly human; they involved man in his universality, man in his entirety, man in his history and in his politics. No one can consider those crimes as a geographical peculiarity or a historical oddity; on the contrary the twentieth century reached its fulfillment in that place; the crimes in Cambodia can even be taken to represent the whole twentieth century.

This formulation is excessive, to be sure, but its very excess reveals a truth: It was in the Enlightenment that those crimes took place.

At the same time I don't believe that. Not everyone is Saint-Just. And taking everything literally is also a crime.

PACKING MY THINGS was easy. I owned one change of clothes, black of course. Also a big spoon marked "US" that my mother had swapped for, two or three days after the evacuation of Phnom Penh. This was a precious object; with a big spoon you could take more food from the communal plates. That was where the struggle began. And finally I still had a white shirt that I never wore and a black hammock that my mother had sewn together from a sheet. Nothing else. The prohibitions were innumerable and the searches incessant. I would never have dared hide anything at all. Before 1975 one of my brothers who was studying in Paris had sent me a lovely pair of gray velvet pants. My mother had made a small backpack out of the material, and into it I put my spoon and my spare clothes. On difficult days, I'd stroke the worn velvet, dreaming about my mother's fingers, her face, her smile, her thoughtfulness. I was a child, and I went about like that, carrying my world on my back.

IN THE BEGINNING the collectivization of property had its advantages—even though there was never any real equality. I remember hating a peasant's son who passed in front of me smiling and carrying two fish suspended around his neck, whereas I was incapable of catching even one. Then the advantages disappeared. There was no more sharing, no swapping, no discussion. It was every man for himself. I saw children die, both puny and not. Adults too.

Human resistance is mysterious: I acted like an animal. I remember burning big forests with other children in order to prepare the land for corn planting; we waited three days for the ground to stop smoking. At dawn, we walked barefoot among the embers. We scratched the ashes and the burned earth with our poor feet, like dogs. We followed our instinct. Don't reflect. Fight. And we found some little animals that had been caught in the fire—squirrels, lizards, snails—and devoured them on the spot.

Later I worked in the mountains. It rained day and night. Snakes crawled from one bush to another. We would find cobras and beat them with sticks. In the end they wound up on the fire.

I'd shiver in my rain-drenched hammock. It was impossible to move. Impossible to sleep. Impossible to talk. I learned to husband my strength. Not to struggle against cold and fatigue, but to accompany them. I didn't think anymore; I was alive.

WHEN FILMING DUCH, I use only two kinds of shots: head-on, and from a slight angle. The setup is rigorous. Austere.

In the very beginning, Duch barely looks at me. He turns around or stares at the opposite wall. I say, "I can't film only your ear! *You're going to have to look at me!*" He jumps. I've got a feeling that the words I've used have some terrible significance for him. In any case he changes his position, settles in, speaks to me. But he casts his eyes upward as if looking for light or ideas. I film him. For hours he talks without saying anything. Then some progress: he recognizes a photograph. But he dodges. Hesitates. Explains in his soft voice that Office 870 (the seat of the Communist Party's Standing Committee) knew everything. In other words, Pol Pot, Ieng Sary, Nuon Chea, Khieu Samphan. He adds, "I'm not paranoid like Pol Pot." To emphasize his passive resistance he rewrites the history of the years between 1971 and 1979, when he was in charge of M-13 and then S-21, "Since I couldn't protest, I shirked." Duch sidesteps. Doles out a few bits of truth. I never try to corner him. But he ends up contradicting himself. Thanks to cinema the truth comes out: montage versus mendacity.

I count up the number of atrocities committed in S-21 that he's alluded to during our interviews. The former "comrade interrogators" from the group called "the Biters" are much more forthright. Their voices are clear, their eyes frank. According to them torture sessions properly conducted were supposed to lead not to death but to a confession. The medical units regularly wrote up brief, cold reports. From time to time a prisoner would be given medical care so that the torture could continue. Photographs of prisoners who died under torture have been found; some of the victims are wearing bandages or wound dressings.

Here are some tortures that were codified and put into practice in M-13: whipping the prisoner bloody; suffocating the prisoner in a plastic bag; thrusting needles under fingernails and then striking the needles with a ruler or stick; electrocuting the prisoner by attaching cables to his ears or genitals; making the prisoner eat excrement with a spoon. And all that continued in S-21.

Finally, there were the rapes, which officially didn't exist. Many known cases took place in S-21. Who can believe that those dozens of young interrogators, cloistered for years in that horrible place, never had sexual intercourse? During the preparation of my film, one of the interrogators explained how he'd tortured a young woman, "I desired her, and so I hit her hard, then harder and harder." He repeated, "I kept hitting and hitting." Then he suddenly stopped talking altogether.

I ask myself questions. Was there a gradation to the torture? Was there a strategy based on fear? Without a doubt, but Duch says nothing about that. He didn't look. Didn't see. Didn't hear. He annotated files in his office. Such was his official position. I quote a line to him, "There's good and bad in all police work." Politics as a free pass. Utility as a tolerance threshold.

ON A PAGE in one confession Duch makes a recommendation, "Moderately harsh torture."

SOME OF THE TORTURERS are themselves denounced in the very heart of S-21. For sabotage. Treason. Rape. The policy of obtaining confessions had no limits. Like all prisoners in S-21, they were photographed—but without the cap each of them is wearing in his photograph as a "comrade torturer." Later their faces were covered. The decline had begun.

Duch also describes the experiments with medications that were performed on the prisoners. And the taking of blood from certain women, a subject I'll return to later. Duch adds, "Transporting corpses is easier."

I LISTEN TO Jacques Vergès, speaking in Barbet Schroeder's documentary film about him, *Terror's Advocate*: "Some people say the genocide was a deliberate crime. To them I say NO. There were deaths; there was a famine; it was involuntary. Admittedly there was repression well deserving of condemnation, and it included torture, but it didn't involve millions of human beings. Besides as far as the number of deaths is concerned, all you have to do is look at the mass graves, et cetera, that have been found, and you see they don't contain anything like the number of bodies people allege." Then he says, "The American bombardments and the famine caused by the American embargo and the American blockade—none of that has been taken into account. The whole thing's been made into a single package and laid on the backs of the Khmer Rouge."

To be sure, Cambodia wasn't self-sufficient before the Khmer Rouge revolution. To be sure, Democratic Kampuchea accomplished its own isolation. But so extensive a famine had never occurred before. When it broke out and didn't abate, why weren't the borders opened and importations begun? Why were individuals prohibited from fishing and picking fruit when famine was devastating the country? Where did our unit's rice production end up? Why weren't the Khmer Rouge personnel hungry? Office 870 was very well informed. Khieu Samphan and his team received regular and frequent telegrams from every region, indicating the production levels attained.

Without blinking an eye Jacques Vergès asserts that there was no "deliberate" mass crime committed in Democratic Kampuchea, that there was no genocide and no organized famine; and to top it all he declares that there weren't as many deaths as are claimed. Was he present in the country at the time? Does he have access to special information through his childhood friend Khieu Samphan, who's currently on trial in Phnom Penh, and whose lawyer is Vergès himself?

Really, though, "all you have to do is look at the mass graves that have been found, and you see they don't contain anything like the number of bodies people allege"? Staring at an image doesn't permit you to write history. And studies from the Cambodian Genocide Program at Yale University list more than 20,000 killing fields over the whole territory of Cambodia.

For my part I persist and say: in Democratic Kampuchea, there was a mass crime *and* a famine. Among means of extermination deprivation is the simplest and most effective, the least expensive, and the least explicit. There are neither weapons nor slogans, neither rice nor water. I've seen oxen eating human remains, bones and flesh together. We were hungry, but most particularly hungry were those who were meant to disappear.

ME: "In S-21 were your men sometimes cruel? Malicious?"

DUCH: "No, never. Neither malicious nor cruel. Malice and cruelty formed no part of our ideology. The ideology was in command. My men put the ideology into practice."

Thus the torturer lives in doctrinal order. He has no emotions, no impulses. To accept these terms is to preserve the torturer's humanity.

When the Angkar took possession of the former psychiatric hospital Takhmao, an annex of S-21, with the intention of turning the building over to the Ministry of Social Affairs—I'm not making this up—Duch had all the graves opened and the bones of the sick and the leprous massacred since 1975 disinterred. One by one. Him Huy was present. The stench was unbearable. Rotted flesh inside shreds of clothing. Then those remains were burned so that the secret could be maintained.

Duch is an ideologue: enemies are waste matter, to be treated and then destroyed. It's a practical task that poses hygienic, mechanical, and organizational problems.

When their hands touch those decomposed bodies, those scraps of flesh, the torturers of S-21 become waste matter themselves, dehumanized in their turn. Nobody escapes submission; nobody escapes terror.

AUGUST 18, 1978. The confession of Om Chorme, twenty-nine, leader of a mobile unit in Region 24. He writes, "I'm in chains. I'm less than scum. My torturer wants me to salute a picture of a dog."

DUCH STARES INTO my camera. "In S-21, the only person who didn't get promoted was me," he says. And he laughs.

WHEN MY MOTHER was a child she worked in the fields in the Mekong Delta. Today I know I'll never know more than that. Nothing of her or her family remains. Everything's been lost, canceled, or destroyed.

From the time when the Khmer Rouge sent her to the rice fields in the summer of 1975, my mother showed she hadn't forgotten her past. She could still winnow rice and grind grain without getting exhausted. She could still "read the wood" in order to split it with one blow of her ax. The Khmer Rouge were amazed: a bourgeois woman who worked like a peasant! The new world held some surprises. Myself, I used to watch my mother for hours, and all the more because my father, for his part, wasn't up to very much.

Everything grew under her hands. She had two green thumbs. She planted tobacco, even though it was forbidden;

she'd dry it, chop it into shag, and then swap it for rice. Or for zucchini or cucumber seeds. She fed us and took care of us and nursed us when we were sick. I owe her my life.

DURING ONE OF the hearings the judge speaks; Jacques Vergès ostentatiously turns his back and looks out into the courtroom. Nobody says anything. Nobody dares to say anything. But everybody *sees*: Yes, the great lawyer is putting on his show. A mockery. Television images. Provocation, tension. Let the humiliation never cease. Let death, followed by the obliterating of death—let all that be a game too.

THE KHMER ROUGE slogans sounded harsh, but they possessed a simple beauty rich in imagery. I remember one of them that we often put into practice: "The property of each Cambodian can be contained in a bundle." There was a thought for every situation—often direct and violent, sometimes harmless or enigmatic:

> *The Angkar has pineapple eyes!* (That is, the Angkar sees all.)
> *If you're a libertarian, if you want liberty, why not die at birth?*

Only a heart without feeling or tolerance can take up a reso-
lute position in the struggle!
The new people bring us nothing but their bellies, which are
full of shit, and their bladders, which are full of piss!
A person suffering from the sickness of the old society must be
cured with Lenin's medicine!
He who protests is an enemy; he who resists is a corpse!
The worksite is a battlefield!
Master the water! Master the land!
The system of dikes in the rice fields transforms your percep-
tion of things!
We must destroy the enemy, both visible and invisible: the
enemy in thought!

In Khmer Rouge Marxism, everything passes through
language. Everything converges on the slogan. It's a
dream of press-ganging the world, of holding it in a
sentence: "The radiant revolution shines forth in all its
splendor." "You must bring everything to the Angkar."
But there was also "Comrade, you have to forge yourself, you have to reconstruct yourself." The old language
hadn't disappeared, but it had been molded into a cold
language, a totalitarian language: a response to the absence of questions.

Our songs evoked combat, suffering, enemies, spilled
blood. In the revolutionary spectacles that were filmed
at the time, and which I watch pensively in my Phnom
Penh office, everything's mechanical, jerky, the opposite

of supple. Lift the revolutionary fist; open your hand to the sky, full of hope; or perhaps swing your fist down hard in a slicing movement. There are no more muscles or bones, no more twists and bends, but instead two or three ideas. The human being disappears inside his edification.

The fist encloses strength. If it's clenched, it affirms, it threatens. It forges the group. It's ready to pound, to destroy: *kamtech*. But if the hand opens, a dove comes and lands on it, pecks at an invisible seed in the palm, and then flies away: it's building a nest of peace.

The Angkar's propaganda images are revealing. A set of them shows Pol Pot calmly walking, his hand touching his *krama* at the left shoulder. Black pants. Black shirt, buttoned up. Sandals. He smiles in the bright sunlight. When he doesn't smile his features are stony, silent. He's holding a fan that he never opens in his left hand. His right hand waves a greeting, as if he were greeting nobody; and after all maybe nobody was there. From time to time, a hand thrust from a black sleeve reaches out, seeking his hand. In the end Brother Number One stops, plants his feet firmly, and gazes at the horizon, which is invisible to us. The power of the marionette.

KHIEU SAMPHAN, in 2004: "How could a person murder someone for stealing a potato? Or for having broken a sewing needle?"

I remember a Khmer Rouge song broadcast over the loudspeakers at the worksite: "You eat roots; you get malaria; you sleep in the rain; and all the same, you fight for the revolution." I can still remember the rhythm and the key. I even think I could hum the song, but do I want to? Or maybe I don't dare. You eat roots. You sleep in the rain. That was our life.

DUCH TALKS ABOUT his "work" in S-21: "I applied myself. I applied myself. I never broke discipline."

I say, "Do you remember the barbed wire on the façades of the buildings?"

He mimes surprise. Barbed wire? No. He saw no such thing. Now when Duch was anxious and depressed, he'd pay a visit to the sculptors and painters—once or twice a day, he specifies. Therefore he saw the barbed wire. We even know that he ordered its installation after a female prisoner's suicide. Killing oneself was prohibited. Killing oneself thwarted the confession, the people's justice, and with it the execution.

His lies and his omissions necessarily end up constituting a negation of the crime. Duch wants it believed that he directed an office filled with files, which he dealt with strictly and seriously over the course of four years, always aiming at truth. A theoretical task: he finds the idea that a "technician of the revolution" could have blood on his hands insupportable. For the tenth time I allude to the howls, the blows, the electric shocks, the men and women in chains, the high walls, the convoys that left in the night with their lights turned off. Duch replies, "You've noticed the way I walk, Mr. Rithy. . . . You know I walk with my head down." Thus he failed to see the yanked-out fingernails, the shackles fixed to the floors of the cells, the blood on the tiles—and the bodies everywhere.

I can't sleep at night. I start awake. And then I read, or smoke at the window. I think about my films. About Duch's statement, "I walk with my head down." I touch the photograph of my father, standing stiffly in his white linen suit. My fingers brush his shirt, his cufflinks. His wrinkled cheek. Faces come back to me. Bophana's. My mother's. Our nameless faces, photographed for the records. I try to dodge my grief. I don't want to fall. Then I wait for the day to come, occasionally checking my watch. Finally it's almost here, morning in Paris or in Phnom Penh, and the living call out to one another, straddle their bicycles, tote their schoolbags, laugh, make signs, exchange greetings; the city smells of asphalt and warm bread, of perfumes and flowers and exhaust fumes; at last I can sleep.

WHEN THE STENCH from the wound in my foot becomes intolerable, I'm sent to the regional hospital. I wait on the side of the road for an hour; then a truck arrives and I'm lifted into the back. We drive for three hours without encountering another vehicle. Here and there, a few oxen. Black-clothed peasants in the middle of the rice fields. Some shacks. Some ditches. We go through the city of Battambang, which like Phnom Penh has been completely emptied of people. We spend the night in an abandoned depot. The following day, we stop at a pagoda that has been converted into a hospital. It was there that I would have my first visions of hell.

The Khmer Rouge nurses first put me on a sort of exterior terrace because I stink so bad. I piss and shit in a pot, right in front of everybody. I wipe myself in front of everybody. I'm an animal. The nurses barely come close to me and complain about my smell. They put on masks before tending my wound. They remove my bandage, tearing off some skin in the process. There's dried blood and pus. I weep, humiliated by their grimaces of disgust.

Then I'm transferred to the former central building of the pagoda, the *vihear* or sanctuary where people came in the old days to pray to the Buddhas. I realize that it's the ward where they put the dying. The smell of iron and disemboweled bodies floats in the air. Some tuberculosis sufferers spit blood. I try to protect my face with my *krama*. They're all dying, one after another. I find that I have a neighbor, a boy my age, whose wound resembles mine: he's received a slicing blow to the knee. He lies stretched out on the tile floor, like me, and moans. His bandage keeps coming undone. Flies buzz around him, and it's hard for him to chase them away. He's less combative than I am. He cries out. He writhes and raves. Very soon, I can no longer bear the company of this double, whose wound gets worse every day, turning black and growing hideous and hot.

I have the sensation that I'm watching the unfolding fate in store for me. I resolve to stop taking naps during the day, because I realize that sleep is a renunciation. I'm waiting for something to happen. I force myself to remain upright on my sleeping spot. As often as possible I go and sit outside, crawling there on my hands, like a legless cripple. I get up at night to tighten my bandage. I struggle to make my way to the shower once a week, assisted by a nice Khmer Rouge doctor. The bucket of cold water on my wound makes me cry out, but it's such a joy to escape the bandages and the blood. I use the occasion to wash my only outfit, which is of course black.

ME: "What is duty?"

DUCH: "It's an order given by one man to another."

POL POT'S VIEW: "No one can do his duty without being faithful to the revolution because that's the most sublime duty of all."

THEREFORE THERE'S no conscience, no interiority. Duch knows only his relationship to the other, and that relationship encompasses authority, submission, and cries of pain. I ask him the difference between "duty" and "mission," and what a "moral obligation" is. He hesitates. In fact, he doesn't understand my question. When you don't believe in freedom and conscience, what difference can you see between "duty" and "order," between "duty" and "mission"? None at all. For the Khmer Rouge there was no political law. There was no moral law. There were no more words.

I'M TRYING TO UNDERSTAND why classification by color was a practice so widespread among our new masters. Was it because many of them didn't know how to read? Or was it the inverse, namely that they didn't want to admit they knew how to read? Vitamins were sorted into different containers and classified as B1, blue; B12, green; C, yellow; et cetera. I remember that the nurses brought in injectable medications in Coca-Cola or Mirinda bottles. The same syringe was plunged into the bottle, once, twice, ten times, and then into flesh. It was quite painful, and the syringe was almost never changed.

I was amazed to find those colors again in S-21, in the big notebooks in the archives. Opposite the name of each prisoner, there's a colored line: Blue meant the subject hadn't been questioned yet; black, he was being tortured; red, the Angkar had obtained his confession. "To spare you is no profit. To destroy you is no loss." That axiom, by definition unprovable, leads to only one conclusion: death.

Duch speaks with pride of the organization he initially set up and then ceaselessly improved. The Angkar shared this predilection for method, which was more important than humanity itself. They methodically classified, ordered, added, or subtracted. It's as if Duch still spoke that language. As if he's never left that world.

It seems to me that the Khmer Rouge were obsessed with numbers and codes: the torture centers that Duch directed (M-13 and then S-21), the hospitals (one often cited is Hospital 98), the battalions (290, 250, 450), the elite unit (703), the office of reeducation (105).

The leaders had codes as well as several names. Son Sen was number 89, but also Khieu. Apparently this practice had begun in the days when the underground and the guerrillas were fighting against Lon Nol and the Americans. The leaders were very difficult to identify (Pol Pot changed his name several times and didn't introduce himself to the world as the number one man in the regime until *one year* after the fall of Phnom Penh); the organizational chart was opaque, not to say nonexistent. The Angkar was all the more powerful in that it was founded on an uncaused order. Few faces, few names—that new world was ruled by codes.

When I submit the S-21 records to his inspection Duch often asks questions and gives answers.

ME: "Who read all those documents? Who received them and annotated them?"

DUCH: "Office 870."

ME: "What was Office 870?"

DUCH (coldly): "The permanent seat of the Central Committee of the Communist Party." As if he finally had to name those who shared the secret.

Later I asked him why the torture center in the capital was called S-21. It was the place's radio frequency. But the former mathematics professor didn't like that number. The reasoning behind his displeasure was as follows: In the jungle, he'd been the commandant of M-13; now, $1+3=4$; four out of ten, that wasn't even half! At the time, he goes on, he didn't know that in Europe, the number thirteen means bad luck. S-21 was worse; $2+1=3$, therefore a whole "grade" lower. Duch was annoyed. I quote him, "I like numbers whose sum is nine when you add them up." Moreover it dawned on him that all the important offices of the Khmer Rouge regime had either a conspicuous code (Foreign Affairs: B1) or a three-digit one: Propaganda, 366; Regional Economy, 307; Communications, 308. Still today he wonders, "Why did the security service have fewer digits than the others? My feelings were hurt."

IN M-13 DUCH spent a little time sleeping and a lot of time interrogating. He examined the palms of the prisoners' hands. When he found one that showed a long lifeline, he'd be surprised.

"I can't believe it," he'd say.

I ask him, "And afterward you'd execute them?"

Duch laughs and answers, "Yes!"

A former prisoner in M-13 tells me that Duch loved the steamed cakes Mam Nay's wife used to make for him back then.

AFTER TEN YEARS under lock and key, during which period his crimes have become well known, Duch calmly informs me, "No one could surpass me in the study of mathematics." Furthermore, he affirms that "no one else had my ability to interrogate prisoners or explain ideology." I believe those two statements form a matching pair. Later comes the conclusion: "We're machines. We're instruments."

ONE DAY a nurse proudly brought us some medicine: a black poultice devised by the "revolutionary" laboratories—I should say "our" laboratories. The nurse cut out pieces of the thick substance and laid them over our wounds. It was a mixture of leaves, resin, and to tell the truth I don't know what else. My neighbor's knee was in such an advanced stage of decay that the poultice, like his flesh, fell off in strips within a few hours. In my case the poultice had the opposite effect; it stuck to my ankle and foot, which had seemed to be holding up rather better than his knee. The following day I removed the poultice, little by little, with my fingernails. It was a mass of glue from hell, a kind of tar under which my injury had grown worse.

Since we knew those medicated poultices were useless, we swapped them . . . for chili peppers. Which proves *a contrario* that some people believed in those revolutionary remedies! Later I saw archived photographs of the Khmer Rouge laboratories where roots, boughs, leaves, tree trunks, and other natural materials were stored and never transformed. It was the defeat of the *Encyclopédie*. Better the old world, elementary, earthy, than cold, difficult knowledge.

We loved hot peppers, which gave some taste to the revolting concoctions we got served, but our little trade deal became known. The deputy director of the hospital summoned us immediately, my comrade and me. We were scared of him. He liked to leave the operating room with red iodine stains on his hands and walk around among us. He found that exciting.

It was evening when the deputy director had us brought—we couldn't walk anymore—to a field bordered by coconut palms, behind the pagoda. There we were thrown on the ground. In front of us, there was a freshly dug trench. We were going to die. Disappear forever. I was crying. From time to time the deputy director shined his flashlight on our faces. We stayed like that, awaiting death, for ages. Through my sobs I implored the man, I implored the Angkar, to pardon us, and I think my tears are what saved us. In the end he had us escorted back to our pallets. His only comment was, "As soon as it's possible, the Angkar will send you somewhere else."

Some days after that episode my neighbor interrupted his groaning, sat up straight, and screamed in terror, "A worm! A worm!" The doctor hurried to him, bent over his knee, and sighed. With some little metal pincers, he extracted a white worm from the boy's knee. A fly must have laid eggs in his flesh. I didn't try to find out any more than that. We knew intuitively that it was all over for him: animal life breaking into human life. He died the next day.

THOSE WHO HAD a little gold could buy anything, especially real medicine made in China, along with vitamin C and penicillin. Gold had kept its value. The Khmer Rouge personnel knew all about it and participated in the exchanges. One part of the country—like my mother, saving her jewels for her children—was preparing itself for the time "after" and making a bet on the future. Regimes pass; gold remains. The magic of old metal. A little religion. Or prudent savings. As for ideology, I believe everyone had forgotten about it. We'd thrown it away, along with humanity.

DUCH'S LAUGH. MANY people have spoken to me about it. An M-13 survivor, whom I filmed on three separate occasions before he died, retained an indelible memory of Duch's laugh. He could even imitate it. I could hardly believe it—it was too beautiful, too easy: Laughter bursts out in the midst of mass crime.

Duch has a "full-throated" laugh: I can't think of another way to describe it. The first time I heard it, it made me jump. He stopped it short. *How can this be?* I thought. *He tortured people, taught others to torture people, indoctrinated torture, organized an extermination, disappeared for years, taught in China, changed his identity, worked for an evangelical humanitarian association, converted to Christianity, and was finally identified and arrested; he's spent ten years in preventive custody and is going to be judged by a criminal tribunal, and . . . he's still laughing?* Yes, the devil laughs at what he calls other people's "lies," namely the admissions of the interrogators and guards, who have acknowledged the torture. He laughs like a child. No, really, he hasn't heard about the man who was electrocuted while strapped to a metal bed. He, Duch, spent four years in a world plastered with file folders.

I'D LIKE NOT TO KNOW anything anymore. Yank myself out of that period, take gentle leave of my childhood. I'd like never to hear Duch's laugh again. Nonetheless I listen to him. I observe him. I approach him. I read a great deal: Gitta Sereny's *Into That Darkness*, about Franz Stangl, the commandant of the Treblinka extermination camp; *Life Laid Bare* and *Machete Season*, two books about Rwanda by Jean Hatzfeld. In the second I read these words:

> The killings were out of our hands, and so is forgiveness. We never properly discussed the killings at the time of the marshes; I do not know if we can talk adequately about forgiveness now that everything is over and done with.

I study Louis Althusser's *For Marx* and some of Étienne Balibar's texts on Marx and historical materialism. *The Origins of Totalitarianism* and *Eichmann in Jerusalem*, by Hannah Arendt. Adorno's *The Authoritarian Personality*. Robert Antelme's *The Human Race*. Charlotte Delbo's trilogy *Auschwitz and After*. I watch hardly any films. I breathe the poems of René Char and Jacques Prévert.

I read some research works on Duch. I know the first
and last names he was given at birth, then the ones a
seer gave him at three months to ward off disease and
evil spirits, and finally the one he chose himself when
he was fifteen. I know that as a child Duch suffered from
the harshness of his French teachers. I know that when
he was twenty his bicycle was stolen, and that he was
very offended. I know that he was madly in love with
Kim Heng, whom he affectionately calls "my frangipani
flower." She elected to study literature; he chose mathematics. He begged her to choose the same field as he did.
"Together, the two of us, with our teachers' salaries—we
would have been able to live quite decently," he says.
"We could have had an average lifestyle." But those
dreams came to nothing. Kim Heng refused. Lost love.
Without saying her name Duch claims he still loves her.
His throat is dry; he drinks a big glass of water and goes
on, "Life is strange. I became a Khmer Rouge, but I
could have been in Lon Nol's clan. Then I would have
been executed by the Khmer Rouge." Lost in thought
Duch rewrites his life.

Rapidly, one after another, his friends are thrown into
jail by the secret police. Then he asks his "master" Sun Sen
for permission to marry Rom, a woman of solid peasant
background, "for class reasons." I know a lot about that.
I'd like to understand. To explain. I'm an innocent.

KHMER ROUGE SLOGAN: "Personal feelings are not allowed."

DUCH: "If someone tries to force me to speak untruth I refuse. I hereby make a final declaration, publicly and for the last time: I never tortured anybody."

DURING THOSE FOUR YEARS I didn't dream. Or my dreams were buried too deep to remember. I have a memory of continuous fear. Emotions, impressions, feelings were forbidden and couldn't be expressed. I know that's difficult to imagine, but that's the way it was. In the new language you no longer referred to a "marriage for love"; you talked of "organizing a family for the fighters and leaders." You no longer said "husband" or "wife," but "family." Duch: "One plus one has to equal two; one plus one doesn't equal one. Or worse one plus one equals zero." Intimate, inseparable love didn't exist. The Angkar forged couples at its convenience—so important a decision couldn't be left up to individuals: "Beauty is an obstacle to the will to fight." Duch tells me, "My theory was worse. Beauty's a sexual instrument."

My dreams returned to me in the refugee camps after I crossed the Thai border. One morning, I woke up surprised: I'd had a dream. I was fifteen years old.

THE DEPUTY DIRECTOR of the hospital in Battambang performed operations at night because of the unbearable heat. In the white-tiled operating room, there was, of course, no air conditioning. The generator was switched on. The neon lights sizzled. Local anesthetic. Operation.

When I arrived at the hospital with my injured foot, there was still a surgeon in the place, a real surgeon, a "new people" who was subsequently executed. He was supposed to train two Khmer Rouge cadres in his profession. A crash course. The two cadres said they were doctors, but they clearly weren't. The underlying idea—that practical experience was everything—was common among the Khmer Rouge, who'd borrowed it from Mao's *Little Red Book*: "There are no more academic diplomas. There are only practical diplomas." Nuon Chea: "The truth will come from practice." The notion was that when the people are free, they have no difficulty educating themselves. It was imperialism that raised up barriers to knowledge.

My big sister was in that same hospital. Since her husband had been a surgeon, she had a good knowledge of medical terms. At the request of one of the two apprentice physicians, she was translating in secret a French manual of surgery that contained detailed sketches and explanations. At night the comrade came to bring her food and pick up the pages she'd completed. But the other apprentice physician disapproved. "We're not servants of imperialism!" he said. "We're more than capable of combating illness on our own! Don't stoop to using bourgeois methods!" One can imagine those purely ideological—I was about to write "purely comic"—dialogues: a farce put on by the dead.

The second apprentice won the argument, and my sister and I were sent back to the village. She had too much knowledge—she was lucky they didn't kill her—and I was rotten inside and out. Later the first apprentice and his wife disappeared, carried off by troops loyal to Ta Mok, "Grandfather Mok," a leading Khmer Rouge general who was also known as Brother Number Five.

I remember returning to the village in a daze, my sister and I, traveling first by truck and then by cart, under the hot, metallic summer sky. We didn't speak. We found our family's cabin. I was going to die. But my mother, who had infinite resources for aiding us, had saved a little gold. I don't know how she did it, but she managed to exchange that gold for a tablet of penicillin. A single tablet. She ground it up and gently sprinkled the penicillin powder on my wound, twice. Very quickly, the pain stopped. My scar faded and then disappeared. Within a few days, I was saved. A real miracle. The miracle of science: a trite expression for those who don't need to believe in it.

I kept falling down. I hadn't walked for six months. The duration of my disability comes back to me all at once, even though I can never remember any date, any reference point from those years. But when a boy is thirteen years old and thinking of nothing but survival, does he think about the days, the weeks, the seasons? Every morning my mother and I walked around an enclosed patch of land. I'd lean on her arm and on the barriers she'd made with her own hands. For the second time, she was teaching me to walk. Every three or four turns, she'd give me a long bean. Raw of course! I devoured it. Little by little I regained my strength.

DETAILS OFTEN COME back to me, images, words. I'm projected into the past. The Khmer Rouge never leave me. When I wake up, I feel my hand running through my hair and pulling out a great handful of lice. Or I get dizzy and have to lie down. Such a morning bodes ill for the rest of the day.

THE FAMINE WORSENED. It makes you wonder why there weren't more revolts or outbursts or something. Physical exhaustion was a general condition. The stupefied country was held in an iron grip by those who had rice on their plates. Or gold in their possession, hidden at great cost, and at great cost exchanged. It wasn't possible to move, express yourself, or act without being listened to, questioned, monitored. There you are, there's your revolutionary: a man who has rice on his plate; and who looks for an enemy in other people's eyes.

One of my sisters, the brightest of us all, was sixteen. Her face swelled up, and then her feet, her legs, her hands. She was thin and swollen at the same time. It was as though she'd been filled with water. At a certain level of hunger, of misery, of sorrow, you don't know anymore what you're dying of. She was sent to a hospital in her turn, the one in Mong, accompanied by my oldest sister, who was always looking for ways to escape the village and find her husband.

Besides me, therefore, the people remaining in the cabin were my mother, another of my sisters, and my nephew and niece. I remember their smiling faces, their small, frail bodies. Their parents were studying in France. My niece was five years old, and she would steal things to eat. She'd disappear from the cabin, without a sound. One night, the leader of our group, one of the "old people," sternly brought the little girl home because she'd stolen some corn from his cornfield. My niece was allowed to keep an ear, but my mother forbade her to eat it.

Watching my niece and nephew waste away from day to day was unbearable. I went to my mother and spoke with great assurance.

I said, "Last night, Papa spoke to me in a dream. He asked you to change some gold for rice. For the kids. We must obey him." It was a lie of course.

My mother smiled at me and spoke softly: "One day those people are going to fall. Everything will have to be rebuilt. That gold, those bracelets, those jewels—they'll be for all of you. They'll help you to start over."

I insisted: "You have to give the children something."

She refused.

Their health deteriorated. I remember my niece gnawing on salt at night—god knows where she'd find it. The girl would cry out for her parents. Her jaw, which was almost always clenched, creaked horribly. My mother tried to slide a spoon between her teeth. I'll never forget their last days, hers and her brother's, the end of two small creatures who asked not for a better world but for a portion of white rice. They couldn't get up anymore. They were so thin that the clothes my mother had made for them swallowed them up. Only their bellies were enormous. I looked at their protruding, threatening little bones. Then my mother and I realized they were past help or hope, and something in them realized it too; they stopped groaning. They fell silent. Their big, dark-ringed eyes drifted, incapable of settling on a face, an object, a thought. They were elsewhere.

One night I felt that the end had come. My niece began to breathe more slowly, more irregularly. I clenched my fists. I wanted to be there, not to be there, to hold her hand, to hear nothing anymore. To see nothing anymore. I remember that her slender torso, with its skin like transparent cloth, suddenly stopped shivering. The little girl hiccupped, as though surprised. And then she died.

THE KHMER ROUGE wanted to mold and shape everything: bodies, words, society, landscape. The varieties of rice available in my childhood—"jasmine flower," "ginger blossom," "pale young girls"—disappeared within a few months. There remained to us only one kind of rice, white and nameless. Later what remained to us was hunger.

In that perfectly totalitarian society numbers were more important than anything. Cubic meters of water, tons of earth, tons of rice per hectare, kilos of fertilizer per individual; everything was gauged. A discrepancy was treason. Everything began with the numbers and nothing had any value except in numbers. It was a reassuring passion.

While looking at films from the Khmer Rouge archives, I'm surprised to discover an image overlooked in the editing or added afterward. Between two ideal and radiant scenes, a child stares at the camera. The child's naked, with spread legs; the arms and hands are small, dry sticks; the camera pans down, and we see the lower abdomen, the outsized, smooth labia, like an infant's: a little girl, then, with an emaciated, cadaverous body; and her big eyes call for help.

A week later my nephew died in his turn. Those two deaths were a terrible blow to my mother, who let my oldest sister bury the children by herself. Grief literally knocked my mother's legs from under her—she couldn't walk anymore. I think it was all too much for her. My mother, she who had always been such a tower of strength, gave up. After how many disappearances and deaths in the family? The Angkar decided to send her, too, to the nearby hospital. There she would rejoin my two younger sisters. The youngest, we'd been warned, was close to the end.

That morning, I came upon my mother as two men were carrying her to an oxcart. The leader, a man I liked a lot, was in a hurry and called out, "We're off to the hospital in Mong!" I was still having difficulty walking. I couldn't catch up. I couldn't speak to my mother and wish her well. I couldn't thank her for what she'd done for me: for my foot, for everything, for my life. She made a sign across the distance, her arms around her two bearers, and called out to me in words that, in any other circumstance, would have been ironic: "You must keep walking in life, Rithy. Whatever happens, you have to keep walking." It wasn't advice. It was an order. My throat was tight. I sketched a gentle, far-off wave. I never saw her again.

MY OLDEST SISTER, the only witness I knew, told me what happened next. When my mother arrived at the hospital, her sixteen-year-old daughter had just died. She was still lying on her wooden board. Her body was lukewarm. Peaceful. The lice were moving down from her head to her shoulders and arms, already looking for another warm-blooded human. My mother drew close and sat beside her darling, brilliant, much-beloved daughter. She didn't say a word. Moreover, from that hour, she spoke no more. But she performed an act from the distant past, an act magnificent in its simplicity, a memory from her childhood in the country. She picked the lice off her dead child.

Nail clippers were found in my sister's clenched fist. She'd been afraid that the Angkar was going to marry her off to a mutilated or disfigured combat veteran, as had happened to some young girls in her group. She kept that laughable blade with her at all times, ready to slash her wrists. But her disease got to her first. I know that her body was buried that same day in the common grave I would later work on.

My mother lay down on the wooden plank where her daughter had died and waited her turn.

I TOOK MY MOTHER'S ADVICE: I walked. I went back to work—did I have a choice? I limped and fell down constantly, in the rice fields, in the canals, or on the dikes. I walked; I fell. I'd get to my feet again and the sky would still be spinning. It was impossible for me to stop. Impossible to drink. Impossible to live. The sequence repeated itself, over and over. My strength was gone, but those words sounded in my ears: "You have to keep walking."

One day with the help of a nylon mosquito net, a comrade and I managed to catch a fish. I'm boasting, he was the one who caught it. He gave me the tail and kept the head, which was richer and more nourishing. Ordinary behavior. I smoked that poor tail with its big scales for two days. At last, I received permission to visit my mother. I put the cooked fish in a little bag and found the same jinxed oxcart as before. The hot sun shone as we rolled toward the hospital.

Once I arrived I asked to see my other sister and was shown a thin, sallow woman approaching with a bowl in her hand. It was her.

"Where's Mom?" I asked.

"She died."

"But . . . where is she?"

"She's buried behind the building. . . . You want something to eat?"

Anger and grief paralyzed me. Our words had been taken away, and our hearts had left with them. I was holding my cooked fish, whose smell was now very strong. It was ridiculous. All my sorrow seemed to imbue the poor creature, which I left for my sister.

I bore a grudge against everyone. My mother's body had been taken away. If a living person wasn't worth anything, what was a dead body worth? Later I would bury hundreds of corpses behind that same hospital, and I always thought about my mother and sister. I told myself I could have carried them, as the young Khmer Rouge girls who were responsible for the bodies of dead women did. I imagined myself opening my arms, bending down, and lifting my loved ones to my chest, giving them a belated moment of peace, of humanity, on the way to the erasure and annihilation of their common grave.

As I was going back to the village, someone called me by my given name, my human name. Rithy! I turned around instinctively—proof that the social beast doesn't die so quickly—and saw a woman running after my cart. It was my cousin, whose father, my uncle, was a filmmaker. She had enough time to call out, "They're all dead!" before her words were lost in the sun.

My oldest sister was in the cabin. I told her about my journey to the land of the dead. How many had passed away in the course of a few weeks? We tacitly decided to separate. We would each go our own way. Very soon I lost all trace of her.

DUCH: "Death is with me night and day."
ME: "With me too, but we're not on the same side."

I READ STATEMENTS given by survivors of the Khmer Rouge regime. Since 1979 there have been a great many such accounts. They impress me with their precision; they refer to places and dates and identify people by their names. It's as if the narrator held all the strands and causes in his hand.

All I have are a few traces. And grief, grief abounding. It's why I love Charlotte Delbo's short texts. I've always thought that the Khmer Rouge regime, while proclaiming the foundation of an egalitarian, well-ordered, profoundly just, and free society and to that end tearing the former society apart, kept everything inhumanly blurred and vague. At any moment any individual might disappear, or in other words, be displaced or renamed or executed. And no trace of him or her would remain. I believe there's a name for that regime: Terror.

In his extraordinary work *The Whisperers: Private Life in Stalin's Russia*, Orlando Figes cites a November 1937 diary entry by the writer Mikhail Prishvin (the emphasis is mine):

> Our Russian people, like snow-covered trees, are so overburdened with the problems of survival, and want so much to talk to one another about it, that they simply lack the strength to hold out any more. *But as soon as someone gives in, he is overheard by someone else—and he disappears!* People know they can get into trouble for a single conversation; and so they enter into a conspiracy of silence with their friends.

A little farther on Figes quotes a remark by the writer Isaak Babel: "Today a man talks freely only with his wife—at night with the blankets pulled over his head." As I've explained the Khmer Rouge would creep under houses in the village to eavesdrop on conversations—or to make sure that the couples created by the Angkar were duly having sexual relations and were not just unions of convenience. A brother and sister in my village were forced to have sex together in front of a witness; they pretended to be husband and wife in order to escape a revolutionary marriage.

MY MOTHER'S EFFORTS on my behalf turned out to be insufficient. I was still limping. The pain began in my foot and filled my whole ankle with fluid. It was impossible for me to work in the fields and cut wood.

I was sent back to the hospital in Mong. Feeling clumsy and fragile, I found myself once again on the wooden planks. Then I discovered that some children were much more resourceful than I was. They'd manage to escape from the hospital for an hour or two. Some would search the edges of the ditches in the rice fields and find wild watercress or roots, which they'd use to prepare soups. Others hunted little geckos, which they'd then cook in ashes and eat—but that wasn't something I could do. One of the children even went about looking for monitor lizards on the branches of the trees.

I'd stay in the sun for hours on end, doing nothing and saying nothing. Without tears, without a smile. My head between my legs. Staring at the ground or into space. I was a complete wreck. At two in the morning I'd awaken with gooseflesh and get up to hunt the fleas that infested the wood of our beds. I also discovered translucent lice, which ate flesh and hid in the folds of the body, in the groin, under the arms, behind the knees. In the middle of winter, by the light of the moon, I'd undress and delouse myself, thinking about my mother beside the body of her daughter. I was sad; I was frivolous. I talked to my lice.

It was my luck to be at an in-between age: I had a child's cowardice and an adult's power of resistance. I wrote "cowardice," but maybe the right word is "guile." Had I been younger or older, I would have died of exhaustion— or under the blows of the Khmer Rouge.

Little by little, I became hardened. My mother had bequeathed me her cleverness, her cunning. I set myself some absurd challenges by way of staying alive. I remember telling myself, *If I get out of this, I'll shave my head.* A few days later we were afflicted by a veritable epidemic of lice, and my head was shaved. . . . Comrade Thy became Comrade Bald. When you don't have a name it's as though you don't have a face; you're easy to forget. My courage grew. I wasn't afraid of death anymore. *Death is a hideout*, I thought. *When you're there, no one can catch you.*

I also learned to dissemble. To not be. I created a persona for myself. I became a sort of idiot. A simpleton. I knew that deep down inside of me, there was a little kernel of life, tough and uncompromising. I put up barriers and retreated behind them.

My transformation surely didn't escape the notice of the Khmer Rouge doctors, who didn't want to keep me in the hospital any longer. I had to return to the village and rejoin my group.

I OFTEN THINK about the French Revolution and the Terror. Was the Terror a separate event? An aberration? An unavoidable consequence? I think about the workshop of history. About what's unforeseeable. I think about impossible comparisons. I think about Saint-Just's words during the trial of King Louis XVI, who was neither a child nor a simple citizen: "Louis must be destroyed, not judged." First of all destroy.

In his *Interpreting the French Revolution*, François Furet writes that the collapse of the Ancien Régime created "a general power vacuum" into which "the ideology of pure democracy" rushed. What's left then of the luminous dawn? Of the first battles in the jungle? Of the first writings in the name of freedom? A great darkness. The driving force of "pure democracy" isn't honor, or virtue, or purity; it's *destruction*. And so pure democracy doesn't exist; it's the absence of man. A mathematical formula applied to history.

THE WORK IN S-21 consisted of killing after having obtained confessions. That was the work and the rule. If you respected the rule, you killed. If you didn't kill, they killed you. That was the rule. A comrade torturer explains, "They gave you the power. And then they put on the pressure." Thus they were able to transform human beings. That paradoxical legalism, that mixture of power and terror, was devastating.

THE TORTURERS LAID down their machetes and their iron rods at the feet of their beds. They were free. Many of them went back to the fields. They herded their oxen and fed their chickens or pigs. They raised their children, who were in many cases ignorant of the way their fathers had spent those four years. What people call reconciliation is a refusal. For my part, I don't accept that fall into oblivion.

Indeed, more than thirty years after the Khmer Rouge entered Phnom Penh, who still knows very much about Democratic Kampuchea? Its duration? Its direction? Its real crimes? Was the regime inspired by Marxism? Was it Stalinist? Maoist? Was it first and foremost paranoiac? How should we consider it, after Stalinism and Nazism?

Historical and scientific knowledge progresses. Important books have been published, translated, discussed. But what can one think about Duch's words? What can one think about Duch himself? What can one think about those young peasants who were turned into killing machines? Maybe we'll have to wait another thirty years for all the archives to be finally opened. For the event to become clear, and for it to enter fully into human history. For it to shed its coat of interpretation, where ideology, numerical assessments, revolution, peasantry, and colonial empire all mingle. We'll be able to know, finally and incontestably, the unfolding of those years. We'll know the ideological foundations of the regime. We'll know the writings of its leaders. We'll know the organization of the massacre. We will dwell in knowledge. Then and only then will I accept the mystery, should it still remain. It will be an object of meditation.

AFTER LEAVING THE HOSPITAL, I was sent to an area near Tonlé Sap lake, where I cut wood and planted corn. Then the heavy rains started and our whole group was transferred elsewhere for more woodcutting. As we moved out the sky looked like a threatening sea. Soon our clothes were soaked and our skin red. I wasn't thinking anymore.

I remember that on the second day of our journey we met some soldiers. They spotted two monkeys in a tree and shot at them with their automatic weapons. The wounded monkey sighed as he held the dead monkey suspended by one hand. The couple rotated pathetically. The soldiers fired again. And their meal dropped immediately to the spongy ground.

How many times was I sent from one place to another in the course of those four years? I stopped trying to find out the reason why; and not knowing liberated me.

And so our village was displaced in its entirety— houses, stuff, herds, flocks, men, women—and transferred to the village of Sre O, where I found my big sister. She was having great difficulties with her three-year-old son, whom I haven't mentioned before. He'd been born deaf and frail. He didn't grow. Badly nourished under the Khmer Rouge and lacking medical care, he'd progressively lost his sight. He could no longer see his wooden toys. He'd grope around vainly for his plate, but the rest of us knew it was empty. He didn't understand what was happening to him. He couldn't see or hear or communicate. He was home alone all day long, because we were at work in the fields. He'd scream in anger and hunger and fall asleep exhausted. Then he'd wake up again and recommence screaming. My sister, much weakened, couldn't take it anymore.

One day a village leader called me out. I followed him along the dirt road, and without a word he showed me my nephew, lying on a wooden plank. The end had come. I drew near to the rigid little body; the look on his face was distant, almost gentle, and I think I was relieved.

The men wrapped him in a jute cloth and carried him away. I followed them, but at a distance. I didn't want to see my nephew buried in the ground. Later on I regretted not having accompanied him to his grave.

Since I myself survived, did I start getting used to the notion that only the strong survive? My sister wept every night. She blamed herself for not having been more patient with her son. But we were powerless.

Ever since that day I've never stopped thinking about my starving young nephews and niece. I don't wish on anyone what they experienced, namely absolute want at the ages of three, five, and seven. And I don't wish on anyone the horror of seeing what I saw: a child I was helpless to keep alive. Not on anyone, not even on the former mathematics teacher who would have liked to get a good grade or a three-digit code for the death center he directed so assiduously.

DURING THOSE YEARS a tin can that had once held Nestle's condensed milk served as our unit of measure. Despite the widespread destitution, such cans (empty of course) were to be found, mysteriously enough, throughout the country. Today I know that a can like that holds 250 grams—about one cup—of rice. Some weeks, when the famine was at its worst, the group I lived with at the time shared rice rations of fifteen and eighteen grams, and later of twenty or twenty-five. I remember this number: twenty-seven. Those few grams of rice per person per day didn't provide the body with enough fuel to work all day in the fields.

At the end of 1977 our hunger was unbearable, but one day we received a quantity of white rice. We were warned to eat it slowly, a little at a time. A very young boy with empty eyes separated from the group, clutching his dented US Army mess tin. I saw his trembling hands. How old was he? Six? Listening to nothing and nobody, he vanished. Two hours later he returned, whey-faced, bent over. His stomach had burst. We laid him down under a tree. He moaned and mumbled. In the shadows I could see his face but no sign of a tear. He died that evening.

KHMER ROUGE SLOGAN: "Beginning in 1980 the Angkar will institute a model society such as exists nowhere else in the world. We'll eat three times a day, we'll live well, city and countryside will be equal, and society will no longer be divided into social classes!"

AT THE START of the monsoon some other boys and I, starving and revolting against starvation, started poaching. We set traps and caught several enormous, shaggy rice-field rats. We'd cook and eat them. One night when the moon was full we saw a fantastically large rat disappear into a hole and decided to flush the creature out. I moved my hand toward the piercing shrieks but withdrew it at once. Was it instinctive fear? Was it the sudden memory of my mother's voice? "Rithy, don't touch rats. They may bite you, and then you'll never have a green thumb! You won't plant anything else your whole life." Of course that's a rural, peasant belief, but that day I stepped aside. I gave up my turn. One of my comrades rushed forward and said, "Let me do it! I'm not afraid!" He thrust his arm up to the elbow into the hole in the embankment, rummaged around, and then violently jerked his arm out; a cobra had just bitten him bloody. He held his wrist and groaned.

His two little brothers were with us, and we all quickly went back to the village. The venom was already starting to consume his hand and would soon spread all through his system. For a day and a night he never stopped writhing and moaning. He vomited blood. His body stiffened, and we were forbidden to go near him. Over the course of a few hours, his skin turned first gray and then black. A healer was summoned. He ground up some roots in a bowl, but that was no help. The boy died that night.

Immediately afterward, filled with grief and hatred, we left to avenge our brother and friend. We prudently dug a trench beside the main hole, and the cobra appeared. It seemed to be waiting for us, impassive and gleaming. It was like a little thread of metal stuck in the earth. We cut it to pieces with pickaxes and went back to the village without a word.

Later on I learned how to kill a snake with my bare hands. When I spotted one, instead of running away, I charged at it; a snake was a crawling meal. I knew how to grab the thing by its tail and whip it violently against the ground several times in a row. You couldn't let yourself think about its coils or any sudden rippling. You couldn't allow yourself to be repulsed. To kill a cobra you have to give it a quick, hard, single blow to the back of the head. Any hesitation is fatal.

Fishing, hunting, gathering were all bourgeois, individualistic activities forbidden by the Khmer Rouge. Only community fishing monitored by the Angkar was authorized, but contrary to what the propaganda images showed in four years I never saw a single fish caught that way. And so my comrades and I acted clandestinely, throwing the cold, golden flesh onto the hot ashes.

We knew that certain activities were difficult to check on: herding, for example. The herdsmen would drive three or four oxen deep into the fields and spend the day there. A cowherd could discreetly collect roots or wild cassava, or find crabs in the rice fields or little fish in the pools, and exchange them afterward. Such activities were, however, reserved to the "old people" or to the Khmer Rouge themselves.

I thought of nothing but survival. And so I ate some round, hairy black tubers and even some raw crabs, hungry and weak as I was. I sucked the juice out of leaves or sweet stalks. I stopped thinking about the world before it changed; Phnom Penh was now uninhabited, and for me it had no streets, no houses, no history. In my sleep I'd see my nephews and niece on the threshold, thin-lipped, holding their breath, their eyes hollow from hunger. I'd see the little deaf-mute screaming.

During the first days of the rain I'd slip a few snails into my pocket, hoping that some kind cook would let me lay them on the coals, for it's not possible to eat snails raw. I trembled to feel the shells in my palm and couldn't wait to put the snails in my mouth. I was an individualist, a traitor, but I was hungry. I held on to those little pieces of flesh that gave me the strength to hold on.

ON THREE SEPARATE occasions during our interviews Duch utters three terrible sentences. I record them together here:

"I was the police in Democratic Kampuchea, which until 1991 had a seat at the United Nations."

"I acknowledge that I was held hostage by Democratic Kampuchea."

"In that regime the problem was the same for all: to live, and not to die."

Let's clarify each of those sentences.

"I was the police in Democratic Kampuchea, which until 1991 had a seat at the United Nations": That is, I embodied official, legal order in a state recognized by the other states in the international community; I discharged my function as a policeman, a function that exists in every state. I was on an elevated level, because I was *the* police.

"I acknowledge that I was held hostage by Democratic Kampuchea": I acted against my deepest will by working for the state, which deprived me of my freedom and compelled me to direct S-21; I too was a prisoner; and I risked my life.

"In that regime, the problem was the same for all: to live, and not to die": Like all Khmers I risked my life; I survived the regime whose victim I was.

From chief of the national "police" to "survivor" is for Duch but a step. He recognizes his elevated, influential position, but at the same time he asserts that he stood on the same side as the victims.

And he returns to the subject: "I was terrorized," he says.

I reply, "But you were an intellectual. You knew a lot about many things. You had the ability to choose. To act differently." Which wasn't the case with a torturer snatched from the mountains of the north at the age of fifteen. Duch's defense is a classic feature of totalitarian systems; all torturers and executioners say they were terrorized. Maybe it's partially true. The torturer may feel fear, but he has a choice. The prisoner has only fear.

LATER DUCH MAKES an admission: "In the past, I thought I was innocent. Now I don't think that anymore. I was the regime's hostage and the perpetrator of this crime."

IN THE COURTROOM Duch called upon his deputy and longtime friend, Mam Nay, to give himself up, to tell the truth. To take responsibility. Duch gave a lecture on the theme of courage and memory. And then Mam Nay broke down in tears and said, "I feel much regret because I've also lost brothers, relatives who suffered under the regime, as well as my wife and children, who also died. I believe it was a chaotic situation. And nothing is left for us, except regrets. Many Cambodians perished under the regime of Democratic Kampuchea. These regrets are shared by many, and to speak in religious terms, it's our karma that suffers from what we did. Today I'm trying to find solace in faith and karma." Mam Nay didn't remember anything anymore: not the torture at M-13 and then S-21, not the executions, not even his visit to Choeung Ek with Duch. Both of them lied under oath. The president of the tribunal added his bit by saying, "These events took place more than thirty years ago, and it's very difficult to remember them. We're only human, and our memory is limited." After that phony exchange, there was no longer any possibility that the truth would make an appearance.

ONE EVENING, SITTING on an embankment, I looked out over the rice fields and watched the sky turning brown, gray, and deep green. Soon it was studded with stars. I was alone. I hummed a children's song. It wasn't the song of Ulysses. No, I knew nothing of Dante. I hadn't read *The Divine Comedy*. I hadn't "sailed forth on the high open sea." I hummed little rhyming snatches I'd learned at school and thought I'd forgotten. I also imitated my departed brother. I sang in a language I didn't understand, where Beatles melodies and Bee Gees tunes mingled. Then, putting my own words to a traditional air, I declaimed my story. I thought about my brothers and sisters. I saw my parents' faces. I murmured their living, human names. I wept. My hands were shaking.

Then I sensed that there was someone behind me. I turned around slowly. A young Khmer Rouge woman was standing silently a yard away from me. There were tears in her eyes. Like every child in the country, she knew that air, which is full of sweetness and joy. I saw her emotion. And then her face grew hard. Her whole body assumed a combat-ready position. "What are you doing there, comrade?" she asked. "Stop singing!" She'd listened to me without taking action, and now she had to make up for doing wrong. Emotions didn't exist. The next day I had my self-criticism session.

I REMEMBER THAT my mother used to repeat softly, every evening, "Where are you today, where are you?" Life's a refrain. She was thinking about my brother, a poet and musician. She blamed herself for letting him leave for the capital. A rebellious adolescent, he didn't have the submissive qualities the Khmer Rouge demanded. But he seemed so happy at the prospect of finding his guitar again!

Every year Khmers of all ages go home for the Festival of the Dead. They pray and carry offerings to the pagodas. Melancholy overcomes me today. I can't sleep anymore. I'm not religious, but the idea that my loved ones had no decent burial is painful to me. My brother set up a stupa— a shrine—for them in a pagoda in Phnom Penh, but I don't go there. How can I explain? The dead aren't home in that place.

And so, after thirty years, the Khmer Rouge remain victorious: The dead are dead, and they've been erased from the face of the earth. Their commemorative stele is us.

But there's another stele: the work of research, of understanding, of explication. This isn't some sad passion; it's a struggle against elimination. Of course such work doesn't raise the dead. It doesn't seek out bad ground or ashes. And of course this work doesn't bring us rest. Doesn't mellow us. But it gives us back our humanity, our intelligence, our history. Sometime it even ennobles us. It makes us alive.

A BLACK SCHOOL NOTEBOOK with squared-paper pages was found in S-21. It contains the notes taken by a "comrade interrogator" in the classes Duch conducted there. The notes are written in black ink. The handwriting is lovely. The use of the Khmer language is impeccable. Parts of the headings are in colors. Everything is orderly. Duch admitted, "Those are indeed my words." I call that notebook "Duch's Black Book." I've often pondered those pages, which I'd like to translate and make known someday. How many major criminals have left a notebook outlining their practices and their ideology? It's a unique, complete testimony, an essential text on the business of the prisoner's dehumanization—and the torturer's disinhibition. When you read those pages, you understand that what's under discussion is a carefully thought-out process.

The detailed notes taken in the February 1976 "seminar," led by Duch, are exceptional.

The reader understands from every line that Duch is a revolutionary on a mission. Fear isn't on the program. Duch will fulfill his mission to the utmost. Never hesitating. He's a doctrinaire and an organizer. He's waging a battle begun in M-13, years before. Not only is he not "terrorized," but he develops his subjects, he transmits knowledge, he gives advice. One could say he's refining his work. He quotes from Sun Tzu's *The Art of War*: "Know your enemy. Know yourself." He explains that the pressure on the prisoner must be continuous—*even when the interrogator obtains what he wants*. Duch's words, transcribed in the notebook: "If you obtain a confession and you laugh and feel glad, watch out. Maybe your enemy has won."

Duch works through long arguments, simple in appearance but heavy with terrible implications. "Politics is fundamental. Political work must always be privileged. Then one moves on to torture. There are various torture techniques. But political pressure must always be applied." In other words, torture, which like death is going to occur in these precincts in any case, has to be politicized.

Duch is explicit: "*Then* one moves on to torture" means that no matter what precedes it, torture will take place.

Some of the things Duch says attest that S-21 was not a police center where the groundwork for investigations was laid but a place where *a story was concocted*:

"The prisoners must be prepared to tell the story of their treasonous lives."

"If the prisoner dies, the documentation is to be lost."

"Gather information, analyze it, make an appropriate decision. Thesis, antithesis, synthesis."

Prak Khan, the interrogator attached to the "Biters" group, is quoted: "The confession should be like a story. It needs a beginning and an end. And the enemy must be working for the KGB or the CIA, or he must be a Vietnamese agent bent on swallowing up our country."

Prak Khan also confirmed that he'd invented some confessions. In order to speed things up. In order to knock off and go to bed.

Before the tribunal, Duch's defense alleged that he'd tried to limit physical torture and preferred psychological methods, which he called "political pressure." But what was "political pressure" in a prison where the cries of the imprisoned sufferers resounded ceaselessly? What was "political pressure" when *all the prisoners* wound up executed? Did it include threats of reprisals against the prisoner's family or loved ones? Yes. Deceitful promises of freedom or leniency? Yes. In all cases mental torture was applied, and then one could "move on to torture." Duch here displayed the type of thinking that fascinated those who met him; the appearance was political, the diction mild, the focus clear. Everything seemed to be the result of thorough consideration.

Unfortunately when this same astute intellectual was conducting his training classes, he became more specific: "A confession obtained through psychology is the lowest kind of confession." Unfortunately he also asserted, "Killing without a directive is forbidden." This sentence appears several times in the notebook and was repeated in front of my camera by the torturers.

A question: Who gave the directives at S-21?

S. MOEUN, a "comrade guard" in S-21, tortured a prisoner to death without obtaining the requisite confession; in his turn S. Moeun was tortured and executed. In Moeun's confession, on page nine, Duch points out, "I went look-ing for him in Region 31 with a group of children."

I ask Duch, "Why that region in particular?"

He replies, "It's a remote area, close to the mountains."

I READ *The Art of War*, and these words of Shang Yang: "To govern is to destroy: destroy the parasites, destroy one's own troops, destroy the enemy."

THE KHMER ROUGE nurses didn't believe us. As far as they were concerned we weren't ever sick. We were lying so we could get out of working. No doubt they had neither med-icine nor medical knowledge. No doubt they felt pow-erless. Or maybe, since they were all country girls, they found us, plaguey "new people" that we were, too sensi-tive. I'll never know. If one of us had "tractor fever" (high fever accompanied by violent shaking), they'd examine us and send us back to the fields. One of my companions died like that, from not having been believed. They didn't believe in "rabbit fever" either, though it was equally im-pressive (fever and total prostration). Easy to fake, they thought.

All they had at their disposal were some brown tablets, the well-known "rabbit scat" produced by the revolutionary laboratories. When I found out they contained honey as a binding agent, I tried to get some at any price, so great was my hunger.

THE HEAD OF OUR VILLAGE had a house. Approaching it wasn't formally prohibited, but it was risky. Especially because the village granary was located in that house. We knew his wife, his children, his sister, his cousins all lived there. We knew they all ate white, firm rice. From time to time I'd see him from a distance, walking with the district head, who was the terror of the villagers: he had gold teeth, he carried two pens in his shirt pocket, and he rode bareback. We didn't get near him because he had a reputation for being cruel and sudden.

Three other boys—one of them a little five-year-old—and I undertook to criticize the situation publicly. We were rather too big to remain in the children's unit, but too young to leave the village in a "mobile youth unit." One evening Pheng, who was of Chinese origin and therefore unloved on principle, spoke up: "Under a genuine Communist regime—under Mao Zedong, for example—all citizens are equal in rights and duties. That's not the case here. We don't all eat the same thing. You don't have the right to eat good rice while we get thin soup. That's not in conformity with the ideals of the revolution. We're the children of the Angkar. We're Communists too. We demand the same food for everybody." He went on, his voice steady, and I applauded him. We were on edge. Worn out by injustice. Terrified by death, which was everywhere: in hunger, in thirst, in the rice fields.

We were right: the people responsible immediately performed a self-criticism. We went to bed anxious, but also happy about the changes to come. What naïveté! At dawn, a man came up and pointed to us: "You three. The Angkar is sending you to the front. Get your things." We left right away, on foot, escorted by two militiamen armed with machetes. Truth is a dangerous weapon. We marched along in silence for several hours.

Pheng didn't want his little brother to stay in the village without him. He would have been turned over to an "old people," because, as the saying went, "absolutely everything belongs to the Angkar." But Pheng fought to keep his brother with him and as a result carried him the whole way, in the crushing heat and choking dust. I admired his courage. Finally we arrived at the camp: four lost children in the midst of dozens of men. All Democratic Kampuchea was a work camp, but this one was particularly harsh. There was no fence and no barbed wire. We were simply told, "You're far away from everything here. Don't try to run away, because if you get caught, you'll be put to death."

A JUDGE'S QUESTION to a survivor of S-21: "How were you able to defecate with your feet tied?"

A lawyer's question to a survivor of S-21: "Did you and the others have mosquito nets?"

In these questions everything's hideous, especially the ignorance. I quit the courtroom abruptly that day, slamming my earphones on a table. Too much is too much. Going, I meet Duch's eyes, and I know he doesn't appreciate my demonstration. I get a "friendly" warning. International criminal justice is not mocked.

AT SUNRISE WE'D LEAVE the camp, walk several hundred meters to our worksite, and start digging. Each of us—adult or child, it made no difference—was supposed to extract three cubic meters per day. Then the quota was raised to five cubic meters. It was dusty work, for which we used shovels and pickaxes, without any earth-moving equipment. Were we digging an artificial lake? No doubt, but the Khmer Rouge never told us anything. Nothing—no canal, no pipe—seemed to lead to the vast, empty pit we made. And I never saw any water in it, except for the big puddles left after rainstorms.

We didn't speak. Speaking wasn't formally prohibited of course; the silence imposed itself. At noon we were allowed a bowl of broth. And in the afternoon we had to produce twenty or thirty kilos of fertilizer apiece: we'd look for the leaves specified on a very exact list, gather them, chop them up, and mix them with certain kinds of dense, rich, loamy soil. I also looked for cow dung or termite mounds, but in vain.

How could a person produce so many kilograms of fertilizer every day, under such conditions? It was impossible, we all knew that, prisoners and guards alike. But you had to accomplish the unreal: you had to work, always; you couldn't stop; you couldn't breathe; you mustn't ever give the impression that you were "sabotaging" the group's "fighting ability." It was a murky universe, where terror and sham mingled. Adults were beaten with sticks on principle, if I dare use the expression; blows rained down on their backs. Nobody verified our fertilizer production, which had been arbitrarily determined in some office—or in the heaven of socialist ideas.

FEAR NEVER LEFT US. It was the only truth. As I looked in vain for plants and friable soil, I'd think about this slogan: "If you don't work hard enough, the Angkar will transform you into fertilizer for the rice fields." Today I think about the bodies of those killed in M-13 and buried under the coconut palms and cassava.

The little boy, Pheng's brother, didn't count. At five years old, he wasn't capable of digging. He didn't do anything; he didn't get anything. His brother cared for him with extreme courage. He shared his single daily ration with him. After digging for hours in the sun, he'd let the little one eat with him.

Rather quickly we pooled our rations and our forces, for that was our only chance of survival. The strongest of us would dig; the third boy and I would carry off the freshly dug earth. When the digger got tired, one or the other of us, alternating, would replace him. Sometimes we'd cheat a little. Not much. By sunset we'd be exhausted.

THE COMMANDANT OF the camp, a mysterious man who wore a broad-brimmed black hat, frightened us. He used to walk around with a German shepherd on a leash, a dog that seemed to have stepped out of a tale. The commandant talked little, spat, rolled cigarettes. I saw him thrust a man to his knees and strike him with a rattan switch after warning him, "If you cry out, I'll hit you again."

In the evenings he'd appear in the huts and bark, "Time to sleep." Many fell asleep at once. Absolute silence reigned until the following morning.

The commandant would go back home on a bicycle. He had nothing to worry about. Nobody gave a thought to escaping. We were starving in the middle of a forest, without strength and without support. How could any of us make his way through a country so completely under surveillance, on roads and paths where no one ever traveled alone? Of course, there were some cases where people escaped, but very few escapees survived.

We'd lost our physical and moral ability to think in terms of freedom. Contrary to what a number of intellectuals (particularly French intellectuals; do they know the rather unequivocal slogan, "The spade is your pen; the rice field is your paper"?) believed or wished to believe, and contrary to the propaganda images, I want to state clearly that we were almost never given any classes. Between the ages of thirteen and seventeen I attended a total of five, all of them literacy classes. Not one more. I was happy for a while. Literacy's coming back! I thought. But we had no paper or pencils. No books, no newspapers, no seats, no tables. No free time. No time for reflection. No lessons other than revolutionary speeches and bloodthirsty anthems.

SOMETIMES WE WENT BACK to the worksite after the last meal of the day. Our orders were categorical. We dug all night. We excavated. We banked up. Was there some urgent reason? We'll never know. We'd go back to the camp in the inky dark, groping our way past the prickly bushes and the rice fields. I learned not to dodge, not to skip aside. On the contrary I walked upright, straight ahead. I faced the world of the "old people." My bare feet grew hard; they too were transformed by politics.

Then dates stopped having any importance for me. Or maybe, after that dreadful year, I just detached myself from them. The past plunged me into death. I thought only of staying alive until tomorrow. *Of not getting killed.* And so I stayed in the work camp for months, a pickax on my shoulder, my hands covered with blisters, toiling at the bottom of that vast, absurd basin. Then, without explanation, we were sent back to the village. I no longer knew anyone there; my sister had disappeared. Her hut was empty. There was nothing left inside, not even a pot. And all the other people I knew had been displaced.

During those four years, the entire country was under tight surveillance. It was impossible to move from one village to another without being spotted and questioned. I presented myself to the leader of the group, who welcomed me; he said I could install my hammock under his house. He announced my presence to the village leader, and so on. My whereabouts were known. The Angkar was my family. I owed it everything. "One must respect the interest of the Party. There's no place for the individual," Duch explains, still incarcerated in his prison of words.

In theory I was provided with food, lodging, and medical care. In reality the Angkar was so strict and paranoid that nothing worked. Nothing. We lacked everything.

After I returned to the village I got sick. I was shitting blood twenty times a day. There was no more regular medicine, and no more "new people" medicine either. I was standing on the edge of the precipice. For the first time, I was letting myself go.

THE LEADER OF OUR GROUP told me, "Comrade, you can't stay here. What you've got is too serious." And he accompanied me to the hospital in Mong. The regime's propaganda images showed men in white coats, wearing gloves and masks, wielding medical devices . . . and smiling. That was all a lie. It's fascinating to see how good that criminal government was at presenting the image of an ideal, egalitarian, united, innovative society, when the reality was that they turned our country into hell.

Night had already fallen when the Khmer Rouge doctor examined me for thirty seconds. Without a word he referred me to the ward that was reserved for the dying. That was my place, with the shaky wooden planks, the beds where men lay curled up, stinking, rotting, wet with feces and blood, covered with bandages and dirty cloths and torn skin. A place of groans and tears. I remember quite clearly saying to myself, *This time we've got a problem!*

I sat down, terrified. A pallid young boy suddenly appeared, wrapped in dirty linen. He said, "You're not eating your soup?" He was right—I wasn't hungry. I was full and empty. I had a permanent stomachache. I shit blood. And then nothing at all. When you're dying, you stop eating. I answered, "It's true, I can't eat anymore." He was convalescing, and he was hungry. I gave him half of my soup. He told me, "You mustn't stay there. If you do, you won't get out alive." And he helped me move. He pulled me up out of death.

I shared his wooden bed in the section where the living were. I slipped my backpack under my head. We slept together, the two of us, shoulder to shoulder. Thus I left the dead zone and discovered some rather nice neighbors.

One of them challenged my new young friend. It's outrageous, he said, you're stealing his ration, and he's so weak, he needs it more than you! Another was a musician; he fed me because I couldn't sit up anymore. He made himself a banjo with some bicycle brake cables. In the evenings the Khmer Rouge would come looking for him and have him play revolutionary tunes on his half-American, half-revolutionary instrument.

My health worsened. I closed my eyes, waiting to die. I'd tell myself, *Go!* But I didn't go. And then a sort of inspiration came to me. I told myself I had to get hold of some *guava bark*. Those words implanted themselves in my mind. Strange, isn't it? It seemed to me that my mother had used guava bark to care for my nephew and niece in former days. I remember her repeating some folk beliefs: "When you break a tooth, someone dies." Or "A guava dream means separation." It was my last chance. I crawled over to the foot of a guava tree not far from the hospital. With my back against the trunk, I slowly chewed several leaves. The young boy found a bit of wood and boiled some water; I added the guava bark and made a terribly bitter, black infusion that ended my dysentery at once. I thanked the guava tree. I thanked my mother, who had already rescued me from the cobra. The stomachache, the blood—they were finished; death was finished. I was saved.

LITTLE BY LITTLE I regained my strength. I was assigned to clean up the dead zone. The air in that part of the hospital was thick with disease, sweetish and corrupting. Every morning I'd approach with a lump in my throat. I was afraid. Afraid of the corpses it was my job to locate, palpate, examine. Was a dead man dead? Could we throw him into the pit? I was even more afraid of those who were still alive, stretching out their hands and opening their blackened mouths. I observed them: I'd been in their place. They didn't know anything anymore; good, evil, clean, dirty, alive, lawful—everything seemed to be mixed up together. Their eyes no longer stared because the world was pitching and tossing in front of them.

I screwed my courage to the sticking point, gripped my palm-frond broom and my shovel, and entered. At first nauseated and then simply busy, I tidied up cloths and unidentifiable waste matter and excrement. I stumbled around in that litter. I acknowledged nothing. Sometimes, when it was possible, I also washed some of the men. They were living in their shit. On top of their shit. I'd curse as I worked, my face buried in my *krama*. Afterward they seemed lighter. By force of circumstances, I grew accustomed to the place, and thus I acquired an occupation: I was a cleaning person.

One morning, to my great surprise, as I was going to pick up my equipment in a storeroom, I came upon a box of medicine, real, old-time medicine. Its name was written in French, which I tried to decipher. Or maybe it was the directions or the dosage—I don't remember anymore. I'd lost the habit of reading French, so I had to articulate each syllable. VI-TA-MINE. Penicillin. But a Khmer Rouge official who'd come up to me silently murmured, "Comrade, you can read French?" I jumped; however by then I was inured. I replied something like "No! No, a few words, if that . . . but not at all . . . not really . . ." He gazed at me at length before saying, "Be careful." And then the nice fellow went away. It was one of the rare times when someone showed me something like understanding. He didn't threaten me. He didn't condemn me. He gave me a piece of advice, me, the cleaning boy.

No one would have dreamed about putting my very meager abilities in French to some use, no one. "Learn to eat and work collectively." What a joke. When I read those few syllables on that cardboard box, I risked my life. Subsequently—I'll never know why—the man who advised me was executed. He was no doubt much too nice.

Later I was assigned a supplementary task, in which I was assisted by two other boys: burying the dead. We observed a lot. Our work was to organize ourselves and prepare the grave. With experience you get to know who's going to die. Death's already there; in the eyes, in the breathing, in the hands, in the whole ravaged body. "He won't be spending the night" was the way we expressed it—horrible, I know, but it's true that death comes during the night. At dawn I'd look in silence for those we'd have to carry away.

There were suppurating wounds. Incurable limbs. Pockmarked faces. Enormous bellies. Feet filled with water. The skin, under unbearable pressure, would crack. Sometimes the foot would be punctured so the fluid could drain off. For cancer cases, we had rice ashes, palm sugar, or grilled hashish. We didn't name the diseases. We didn't know them; it was as if the whole country had been afflicted by phenomenal plagues. Only death seemed certain.

I remember a man who was eaten away by cancer and suffering terribly. He was very dignified, but in the end, he begged us: "Do something! Try . . ." His wife was beside him. The Khmer Rouge doctor said vaguely, "We'll get some stuff out of his stomach so he'll be in less pain." As good as his word, he thrust his scalpel into the patient's naked lower abdomen, and pus spurted everywhere. For a few hours, the sick man felt better. Then, all at once, he died. I could tell that the doctor was sad. The wife worked for a while in the cancer ward before being sent back to her village.

THE HYGIENIC CONDITIONS were beyond imagination. There were no surgical gloves and no surgical masks. Instruments were boiled, for lack of any better method. We sharpened the needles. The anesthetics were local and very imperfect. How could it be otherwise, when you've humiliated, displaced, sent to the fields, and executed those who had the requisite knowledge? This lunatic policy is explicit in a Khmer Rouge film from the archive: some smiling, very young children are driving steamrollers; others are working on little power stations or bending over laboratory tables. (Read: child's play!) Whatever a child's origin is, he can do the work. We Khmer Rouge are in touch with the world of matter. It's social practice that gives us our knowledge. (Read: the class society took it away.) Unfortunately Democratic Kampuchea showed chubby-cheeked children mastering technology, not a physician trembling in the night with a scalpel in his hand.

When East German cameramen entered Phnom Penh in January 1979, years after the fall of the city, they filmed an entirely empty capital. Nothing seemed to have changed since April 17, 1975, and for good reason: the inhabitants had left and never returned. The German film presents a trip through the city, a long, unreal, melancholy crossing.

It could be a sublime work if it didn't implicitly depict the country's tragedy. Where are all the humans? The camera enters wrecked apartments or, worse, houses in perfect condition, with tables set and the contents of formerly full plates devoured by rats. Farther on water faucets that were never turned off. Half-fallen wooden shutters bang against the street outside. Here and there banana trees are growing up out of the asphalt. A city garden. The hospitals and laboratories are devastated. A body floats in a yellowed bathtub: the body of a victim? The subject of an experiment forgotten in its formalin?

THERE'S A LARGELY obscure matter, taboo among the torturers, that deserves a history dissertation all on its own: the forced, total taking of blood. Or, to be more precise, the practice of completely removing a prisoner's blood, necessarily involving his or her death. A human being considered as an envelope of flesh, a bag of blood. As an instrument. We don't know details about the process by which these heinous operations were carried out. Another unclarified question about S-21 concerns the method used to execute children. Here, perhaps, we're face-to-face with two areas of investigation that survivors—namely the torturers and executioners—find impossible to talk about. I'll add a third: rape.

Duch acknowledges some instances of "total blood-taking" (I'll use this expression from here on). Sours Thi, the head of registers, refuses to reply to my questions, and the tribunal doesn't question him on this subject. However the notation "blood" appears dozens of times in the meticulously kept registers. One must assume that the blood thus obtained was to be used in treating wounded soldiers from the Vietnamese front. What's certain is that this method of killing people was organized and barbaric.

The blood-taking reveals another of Duch's obsessions: purity. Thus he maintains that he subjected "educated women" to his total blood-taking policy. He gives the example of a young teacher who had voluntarily returned from France—no doubt wanting to participate in the great outburst of popular fervor. Across from her name he underlines the word "blood," which he himself wrote in blue pencil at the time. Coldly Duch explains that in view of the course of her life, it was concluded that she'd "had no flirtations." Was the necessary deduction, therefore, that her blood was "pure"? That she was, in her way, a Khmer princess? A *Mona Lisa*? But if she wasn't, was there a chance of her soiling a fighter for the cause? I don't understand. Was she "pure" because of her intellectual career? Or because she had known no man? And why was blood taken mainly from women?

IN THE KHMER ROUGE revolution, the great body—the people—must be brought together, unified, homogenous, so much so that each individual must be indistinguishable from every other. Therefore, the people had to be purged of its enemies: imperialists, Sino-Cambodians, Vietnamese, Cham. But the fight against the other hidden in the body itself was unceasing. The "technicians of the revolution" thus identified an alien, harmful group of people within the great body of the people; these "others" were the "new people." They formed, in fact, a foreign body, a part of the people that had become the people's enemy. They were a limb that needed amputation. The invention of a group within a larger group, of a group of human beings considered different, dangerous, toxic, suitable for destruction—is that not the very definition of genocide?

AS ALREADY MENTIONED, the conjugal unions arranged by the Khmer Rouge bore witness to the same obsession with purity. Individual consent didn't exist. A woman and a man didn't have to consent. Since the only possible passion was revolutionary passion, matchmaking was the province of the Angkar. Selecting couples for marriage didn't only entail knowing their histories and arranging their lives; it was also a way of keeping them inside the circle. It assured their purity as well as that of the generations to come.

Thus Duch had four children: two while he was the commandant of S-21, and two after the overthrow of the Khmer Rouge, when he was in hiding. In the midst of the screams, the blows, the confessions, he made love to his wife. He caressed her. Eventually he observed her growing belly. She gave birth, assisted by the certified nurse whom Duch kept with his family during all those years. He took care of his children. He showed them the future.

Without batting an eyelid, Duch explains, "I wanted to continue my lineage."

I MEET A Khmer Rouge cameraman, Lor Thorn, who tells me the story of how Pol Pot sent him into the remote provinces of Mondulkiri and Ratanakiri. Later I find the mute images he's described to me, and I edit them in accordance with his indications. It's the construction of a myth.

In the Jarai and Bunong minorities of those provinces, Pol Pot discerned a primary, original, integral Communism whose existence predated the Kingdom of Angkor. He discerned it, revealed it, invented it.

These people did without money and shared everything, including whatever food they harvested or hunted or fished. They stood together. They were pure and far removed from any ideology. Pol Pot had so much confidence in them that he chose his personal bodyguards—his "messengers"—from among them.

The film shot by Lor Thorn and his crew shows members of these minorities planting rice in the soil of a large, burned forest. Then the camera enters an old hut: Pol Pot's. An oil lamp, a ceramic tea kettle, a rustic bed; above the bed, a big map of Cambodia. Even in his sleep Pol Pot thinks about his country.

Under the bed: a wooden bunker. The camera lingers on a pistol hanging from a beam. If the enemy comes, Brother Number One will fight to the death. On the table: books by Marx, Lenin, and Mao—brought by the film crew, Lor Thorn explains. And finally, on the wall the hammer and sickle, surrounded by portraits: Marx, Lenin, Stalin, Engels. The revolution is born in the homes of the pure. In a hut.

WHILE HE LIVED in Paris and was active in Marxist circles, and after his clandestine return to Cambodia, Pol Pot signed his political columns "Pol Pot, Khmer by origin." Purity, always purity.

IN PARIS I GO for a blood test in a laboratory run by a man of whom I'm very fond, a Jewish physician who lost family members in the Nazi extermination. He's generous and melancholy. We understand each other. We know that there's a great human enigma on which we both depend. I tell him I've filmed hundreds of hours' worth of interviews with a major criminal, a doctrinaire, methodical man who often lies, who still talks in the language of the Khmer Rouge period, and who remains a mystery as great as the regime he claims adherence to.

After a moment I add, "Doctor, I think I'm in a depression." He encourages me. My story is a difficult one, he says, but I have to go on. I suffer too, he says. We all suffer the way you do. Forgetting is impossible. Understanding's hard.

We talk about the cinema and history. I explain how I prepare the editing of my films. I work out themes, I screen hundreds of hours of rushes, including those for *S21*. While I'm talking, he's drawing my blood. Suddenly I'm paralyzed. I'm trembling. I can't breathe. I grab his hand, on the verge of passing out. He stops everything and takes me to a café, where I swallow hot tea and sugar. It takes me two hours to recover, but I don't understand; up until now I've always felt good in that man's presence.

SO I HAVE a revelation: Duch has entered into a moral contract with me. A contract of sincerity. He's got me.

From that day on, everything gets away from me. I sleep little. I breathe badly. I have dizzy spells. I stop taking subways and buses. At night I sit in front of the television

set and channel-surf. I'm caught up by the flood of images, caught up and rested. I fall down. I sit up. I open my
eyes. I call for emergency medical help; the doctors find
nothing wrong with me but anxiety. Then I read over my
notebooks: on the day I got sick, I was working on the
blood-taking in S-21.

I wind up discussing all this with a psychiatrist friend,
who tells me, "No, Rithy, no, you don't have a contract
with that man. You don't owe him anything. He's never
acted in sincerity. You're free."

Then I begin to edit my film. I edit the images and the
sound. I cut him off. Duch reinvents his truth in order to
survive. Every act, however horrible, is put in perspective, subsumed, rethought until it becomes acceptable, or
almost so. I edit my film, therefore, against Duch. The
only morality is the editing, the montage. I think about
what he said to me: "In every lie, there's some truth. In
every truth, there's some lie. The two live side-by-side.
The most important thing is that the prisoner denounces
his collaborators."

OFTEN, IN THOSE four years, I'd wash myself while fully
clothed. I'd crouch down and pour a bucket of water over
my head. Or I'd step into a river. I'd scrub my clothes, my
neck, my hair, my ankles, my feet. I'd dry in the sun. And
that's how I got clean. I never used soap or toothpaste.

Nothing belonged to me, not even my nakedness. Or, if I may say so, not even our nakedness, for I don't remember ever seeing a bare, living body. Neither do I remember seeing my own face, except for reflections in water.

Only an individual has a body. Only an individual can look out from inside his body, which he can hide, offer, share, wound, bring to orgasm. Control of bodies, control of minds: the program was clear. I was without a place, without a face, without a name, without a family. I'd been subsumed into the big, black tunic of the organization.

PRAK KHAN: "For the blood-taking, prisoners were brought to the doctors' house, which was across from the entrance to S-21. They were handcuffed to iron beds, blindfolded, and gagged. Then a vein in each arm was punctured and tubes inserted that led down to blood bags under the beds. I asked the doctors how many bags of blood they took from each prisoner. Four bags per person, they told me. Once the blood-taking was completed, prisoners were placed on the floor next to the wall and left there. Their breathing sounded like crickets chirruping, and their eyes were rolled up in their heads. And not far away, their graves were being dug."

IN THE HOSPITAL, we'd use a bucket of water to wash a deceased patient's bed, and then we'd go out into the already white-hot sun to prepare the grave. It would be closed that very evening, for we had neither antiseptic nor quicklime; the stench was unbearable, and we feared epidemics.

Inside in the ward we had to spread out a jute hammock—the same one was used for weeks—carefully lay the corpse on it, and transport it in this fashion to the grave, which was behind the hospital. How many times did we go down that horrible path? My two sidekicks and I were nauseated by the odor. By the flies. By the soil. Death dirtied our hands. After a few days the bodies would swell up, causing fissures to appear in the earth.

One evening without getting undressed, we sprinkled one another all over with alcohol, choking as we did so. I remember that dry liquid, which made our clothes stick to us and burned our eyelids.

We walked barefoot everywhere, in the ward where the dead and dying were, in the hospital, along the edge of the grave-pit. We worked bare-handed among the sick, in filth and fug. But disease spared us. We'd grown tough. Sometimes we'd pass sick people walking from ward to ward. Many of them were lost, shivering, vague-eyed; some leaned on canes, while others sat down, never to rise again. It was a phantasmic world. Nothing seemed completely alive.

Behind the hospital, the graves were distributed over a large plot of land. The plan we followed was fairly exact. Children, men, and women were buried separately. By dint of digging and filling in, we moved farther and farther away from the building. The Khmer Rouge quickly planted green beans, cucumbers, zucchini, and pumpkins on the covered graves. I remember the pumpkins' incredibly long yellow and gray roots, which like us ran out a little farther every day. They taunted us. Decomposing corpses make excellent fertilizer, as implied in the Angkar slogan I've already mentioned. When I found pieces of pumpkin in my soup, I felt nauseated. I could see their roots plunging into soil sown with bones.

Twenty years later I drove past that hospital in a car and learned that the United Nations Transitional Authority in Cambodia (UNTAC) had a big worksite there. I got out of the car and approached the site. Excavators had dug a lake out of the very piece of land where the graves had been. I said to the village head, "But this was a cemetery. Hundreds of people were buried in this place. I worked here." He replied, "Yes, I know. We find a lot of bones. What can you do?" The lake had been dug—more rapidly than with shovels and our muscles, that's for sure—but the water had never had a good color. It remained a thick, taciturn green. No one ever uses it: not for animals, not for crops. Not for drinking. It's dead water.

THE FACES OF THE TORTURERS. Obviously I've met a certain number of them. Sometimes they laugh. Sometimes they're arrogant. Sometimes they're agitated. Often they seem insensible. Stubborn. Yes, torturers can be sad too.

I think about a guard who never tortured anybody. He entered S-21 at the age of thirteen. After some time had passed, he asked Nath, the painter, to produce a little drawing for him, and he made a list of the things he wanted to see in the picture, which would represent his entire childhood: a hut, a rice field, some coconut palms, two oxen, a fishnet. He missed his village. During breaks he'd lose himself in his melancholy visions. From time to time he'd doze off. Huy would awaken him roughly, "Watch out, comrade. Don't let it happen again . . ." Whenever he felt fatigue overcoming him, the terrified young boy would lick crushed peppers and salt. Today I see in his eyes the child he never was.

The torturer's face: lost amid the images that none of them explicates, as if there were an insuperable boundary. The unnameable. And I ask no questions. So that I won't have to relate the answers afterward. So that the human part may remain: it's up to them to find the way forward. But they say nothing about the rapes. They give no details of the tortures. They say nothing, or almost nothing, about the children.

QUESTION: "Why were the prisoners afraid of you?"
ANSWER: "Because they were chained up."

I ask another the same question.

ANSWER: "Because I was the guard and they were the prisoners."

Again the same question.

ANSWER: "It was the guard's duty to be vicious. How can you think they could protest against me?"

The simple world of obedience. Chosen by Duch when they were thirteen, snatched away from their families and their villages, instructed in suffering and death, they knew nothing but order. "Their cultural level was low," Duch explains, "but they were loyal to me." Later, he says, "Those who weren't peasants by origin hesitated to kill. They wouldn't do it with their own hands. But illiterate peasants—if you required them to kill, they'd do it. They'd do it with their own hands." He repeats, "With their own hands." They were tools. They constituted the hand of the revolution itself, a hand that wounded, killed, and didn't tremble.

IN M-13 A YOUNG GUARD, Khoan, interrogates Sok, his grandfather.

KHOAN: "Do you recognize me?"
SOK: "Yes, you're my grandson."
KHOAN: "What do you call me?"

SOK: "My grandson!"

KHOAN: "Your mother's cunt! You're an enemy and you call me 'grandson'?"

Khoan beats Sok with a stick. Sok starts shaking, implores him, calls Khoan "Sir" and then "Big Brother."

KHOAN: "Yes, that's right, you must call me 'Big Brother.' I'm young, but I'm older than you in the revolution."

That young guard, today a man of middle years, appeared as a witness in the trial of his former master, Duch. But he neglected to mention his grandfather.

PARIS. BOOKSELLERS ALONG the Seine. I buy a collection of poems by Jacques Prévert. I sit on a bench and turn the pages. *Cheveux noirs.* . . . There it is. I recite it in a low voice, my father's voice.

> *Cheveux noirs cheveux noirs*
> *Caressés par les vagues*
> *Cheveux noirs cheveux noirs*
> *Décoiffés par le vent*
> *Le brouillard de septembre*
> *Flotte derrière les arbres*
> *Le soleil est un citron vert*

(Black hair black hair
Caressed by the waves
Black hair black hair
Disheveled by the wind
The September fog
Floats behind the trees
The sun's a green lime)

I can feel his hand on my head. I inhale his smell. My father won't be coming back. The Paris sun is a green lime. I get up. I leave the poem on the bench, and the book to be caressed by the waves.

SLOGANS DO OUR THINKING for us. Victor Klemperer thought that language, freely spoken, both arises from and creates the culture. But what's a "freely spoken" language? The language of the Khmer Rouge was always a decree or an order or a threat. And what language does Duch speak these days? Moreover what do our words mean to him?

I ask Duch to name some historical figures he'd like to emulate. He replies, "I'd like to have been Pierre Curie. I admire Pierre and Marie Curie. Kim Heng and I could have been such a couple, but I didn't have the ability." He also admires Gandhi: "I love to look at photographs of him in meditation, with his eyes closed and his hands on his knees. The essence of calm. And wisdom." He even tells me an episode from Gandhi's life—whether it's true or not makes little difference: Gandhi takes a train that goes off the tracks. Many passengers are victims; people search the wreckage for the injured. Screams and suffering everywhere. Amid the nettles where he landed after being thrown from his carriage, the sage is found, eyes closed, in prayer.

KHMER ROUGE RADIO broadcast: "We have defeated our external enemies, particularly the Americans. Internal enemies remain, however, and now we must defeat them too. We must also defeat the enemies that have no visible form: the imperialistic habits of our hearts."

DUCH SUDDENLY SEEMS to remember. The woman who was "operated on alive"—in fact, dissected alive—was Mrs. Thach Chea, wife of Lon Nol's former minister of education.

I CONTINUE MY father's work. I'm an intermediary. I pass on knowledge. I've sacrificed everything to this work, which is taking away my life. And I can't get used to it, not to the images, not to the words. I think about the boy, same age as me, who was so thirsty he'd drink the water in the rice fields at night, and who swallowed a leech. I remember Huy, Duch's security deputy, who refused to acknowledge that he'd killed hundreds of people in S-21. I questioned him at some length, and in the end, speaking curtly, almost mockingly, he said, "Tell me, do you want a number? How high?" I think about Duch, who asked me whether I was going to meet his mother. When I replied, "No, I'll leave her alone, I don't want to see her, all the questions I have are for you," he looked astonished.

I think about Khieu Samphan, the general secretary of Office 870, who claimed to have learned about the genocide from my film *S21: The Khmer Rouge Killing Machine* and asserted that he'd known nothing: "Without minimizing the crimes of the Khmer Rouge, it's imperative that the problem be examined in all its complexity. We have to understand it so that we can liberate the younger generation from the contradictory stereotypes to which we became accustomed." I think about Nuon Chea, Brother Number Two, who dared to say, "I don't know where Tuol Sleng [S-21] is. I've never received a confession. Besides what was this Tuol Sleng? I don't know. At the time I never went down that way. Not now, either."

As I grow older I feel more and more fragile. I don't distance myself: I can't. And I don't want to. Or rather I keep myself at a human distance. I want to be able to *touch* my subject. I have no weapon, no bayonet, no fear, no desire. If I reach out my hand, I can touch the man.

JUNE 20, 1977, in S-21:
  253 executions
  225 men
  28 women
  3 trucks
  2 graves

I BECAME FRIENDS with my two fellow gravediggers. Ours was a genuine, sincere friendship. A rare thing in that period of absolute control, of denunciations, of injustice without cause, of paranoia. No doubt the sweat was necessary, and the weight of the corpses we threw into the earth, and the diseases that grazed us and made us itch, and the odor of death I'm still vaguely conscious of today; no doubt all of that was necessary for us to have bonded so strongly. Pickaxes in hand, barefooted, we almost never walked; we ran among the graves, sometimes unable to avoid them. The soil was very friable, crammed with bones and sinking down into hollows. Decay lay in wait for us. And vermin.

I WORKED ALL THE TIME, and I was always hungry. In the area of the hospital it was my job to clean, I came across a sick man, and I could tell he was going to die quite soon. I suggested that he give me his half ration of soup. He refused, and I thought, *too bad*. In the end, though, when I passed near him again, he said, "Take it!" I carried off his bowl and settled into a spot some distance away from him, but I wasn't able to swallow a drop. Not one drop. I was ashamed.

In a previous, similar situation a boy had offered to share with me and practically saved my life. I say "practically" because the guava tree was my real salvation, no sharing involved. But the boy shared his bed with me. He pulled me back onto the side of the living. His gesture was decisive. When the episode was repeated, I was on the side of the living: I thought about that very sick man, and it seemed to me that I wasn't taking very much away from him (he was near death and wasn't hungry), but I couldn't swallow his rice soup. That day it was my father who guided me. My father, free and alive because he hadn't eaten. And I exchanged some food he wouldn't have wanted anyway. I gave the sick man back his bowl; a few days later he died.

WE STACKED UP the corpses in the common graves, head to head, foot to foot. Sometimes, to save room, head to foot. Or in profile. Twenty bodies per grave during the worst period. But sometimes just one or two. Ghastly arrangements of bones and skin. I'm haunted by the sound a human body makes when it smacks another human body. I use the word "smacks" on purpose, not "strikes" or "bangs into." It's a very particular sound, a kind of dull thump—I don't know how to describe it. A little sound like green wood. The bodies were nothing but bones, no fat, no flesh; everything was skeletal and tormented and hollow. I learned how a human body falls. And in my nightmares, still today, I hear that sound.

Here's a question I've often wanted to put to Duch: "Are you familiar with the sound a human body makes when it smacks another human body?" But I've never asked him that.

He murmurs, "I pity those who died. I pity those who killed too. Personally I couldn't do it." A guard told me the same thing, word for word: "I pity those who killed too."

IN DUCH'S WORLD everything's logical. Everything's in its place. Everything's classified: old or new, destroy or keep, kill or be killed. Even pity has two facets. It's a world of pure ideology, where sincerity isn't a goal. When prisoners in S-21 had confessed under torture and were being led blindfolded to their death, they were told they were on the road to their village.

Duch searches for innocence in horror. He's able, there-fore, to assert that he's "a hostage of the regime and the actor in this crime." In other words, "even though I was the actor in this crime, I'm innocent"; or in still others, "would you have done better?"

Duch speaks in slogans; everything seems smooth, equivalent to everything else. Nothing weighs much. One could take what he says as words of wisdom, as aphorisms. Certain words disappear or overlap. They slide, as though on runners. Duch declares, "The hero is the man who's not afraid to die." Then he goes on: "The hero is the man who's not afraid to kill."

When he stumbles on a word, when a phrase escapes him, Duch stops cold. And then starts over. Every sentence must be *accomplished*. Is this a political habit? Is it caution? The discourse is over.

THE PRISONERS IN S-21 were given almost nothing to eat. They grew weak. Suffered. Shook. They were beaten constantly. All resistance, all humanity had to be broken.

When he arrived in S-21, the painter Nath told me, he had no bowel movement for almost five days because of the lack of nourishment. He started fainting regularly. Some comrade torturers tell me about putting a prisoner on an electrified bed. Then, after several hours of cruel suffering, they brought him back to the common room.

AT THE AGE of eighteen, I discovered Alain Resnais's film *Night and Fog*. I was surprised. It was the same thing. It happened elsewhere. Before us. But they were us.

I REREAD THESE PAGES. I'd like to erase my childhood. And leave nothing behind: not the words, not the pages, not the trembling hand holding them; not the warm paving stones in the entryway where my mother waited; not the spirals; not the dizzy spells. There would be nothing left except Duch and me: the story of a combat. I've filmed his oversights and his lies. His hand, wandering over the photographs. His forceful, sudden respiration, as if the exaltation of former days were still there, in his lungs.

At the age of thirteen, my only thought was to hold out, to survive. And today?

I WAS DUBBED "Doctor Kid." I washed floors. I buried bodies. I assisted in operations. I lived between the children and the adults. Between the living and the dead. I saw things it's impossible to forget. I'm giving an account of them here for a simple reason: I must understand and remember. I mustn't stop trying in the name of propriety—or worse, in the name of ideology.

One day I heard cries coming from the operating room. As my status authorized me to do, I went to see what was going on. There in the room a young woman was writhing in agony. She'd turned scarlet, and she was holding her stomach, which was rigid from her efforts. She'd started to give birth, but the baby presented badly and wasn't coming out. The young woman implored us: "Please, help me . . . save me . . . save us . . ." I can't make myself forget her inhuman screams. Another young woman, a Khmer Rouge doctor, was examining her. To operate or not to operate? She hesitated. The instruments were waiting in boiling water. In hindsight I suppose a cesarean section wouldn't have been impossible, but the doctor did nothing.

Everyone knew that a real doctor lived in the neighboring village, but he was a "new people." He should have been sent for. Nobody wanted to do it. Or nobody dared. The idea of having recourse to a member of the despised class could not be borne. Death was preferable to renouncing an ideal.

And so the staff withdrew and left that young woman to die alone. It took hours. She didn't sleep. She didn't drink anything. She lay groaning with her legs spread wide, deaf to all words and heedless of any gesture. I remember her hands, swollen by tension and fear. I remember her stomach—eventually she began to strike it. Her blood throbbed in her throat. The young woman was dying, together with her baby. All at once, her groaning stopped. She grew stiff, and some young nurses hastened to stuff her into a jute bag. The young body, scarlet and deformed, was ideology itself. The nurses buried it without delay.

⁓

DUCH LOOKS AT A PHOTOGRAPH that shows him behind a microphone. "Look at my face!" he says. "That's not a sad face; it's the face of someone eager to explain the essence of his language. The language of killing, of uncompromising firmness, of the dictatorship of the proletariat—I was the one who disseminated that language in S-21. Anyone the Party arrested had to be considered an enemy. No hesitation! Those were the Party's words. The Party guides you! It's me! You're hesitating? Why? The Party guides you! The Party is me!"

He throws his head back, his eyes on the ceiling. "Excuse me, I'm showing off," he says, and he laughs. Once again, he's laughing. Modesty. Pride. A strange confession from the boss he didn't want to be.

He shows the same pride when he mentions Koy Thourn, the minister of commerce, whom he "treated" personally and in the most complete secrecy. I filmed Duch several times as he spoke on this subject, and every time he proudly explained that he hadn't tortured Koy Thourn physically, he'd defeated him with words—in political combat. What won was the idea: the body of doctrine that organized the society, with its commandments, its slogans, its goons. We were living in doctrine.

WE KNEW THAT there were several young cannabis plants growing behind the hospital; cannabis was one of the few available analgesics. At night we'd steal a few leaves, dry them over a slow fire, and smoke them to forget death.

One evening a Khmer Rouge doctor arrived with a mosquito net filled with little fish. We didn't ask where they'd come from; instead we quickly prepared a soup of fish . . . and cannabis! But I must have gone over my limit because at the end of the meal, I went to pieces. For no reason I began to laugh and laugh, incapable of speaking or of containing myself. The director of the hospital in Mong was Comrade Roeun, who liked to show us his bloodstained hands in Battambang, and who had led me to the edge of a communal grave. Now he came up to me and said, "Comrade Bald, what's going on? Why are you laughing like that?" I kept on laughing, laughing and weeping. He understood and turned, mightily displeased, to the group. Who gave him the cannabis, he wanted to know. Who? Everyone lowered his eyes. There was a great silence, interrupted by my idiotic giggling. I heard myself laughing all alone, and I heard a cold interior voice telling me, *Stop! Or it's all over for you!* It was the voice of my conscience. . . . But by then my laughter had become mechanical, hallucinatory, in the literal sense of the word. The director began to shout: "Get him out of here!" Everything was getting on his nerves—my laughter, the others' silence, the individualistic disorder, the uncontrollable pleasure. I stumbled to my hammock. I was still laughing, but I was trembling too—and terrified.

I REMEMBER SEEING a flash like a metal reflection in the sky one night. Something parachuting toward me? I had a waking dream: a benevolent power was sending me a camera. *This is for you, Rithy, so that you can capture what you see, so that nothing escapes you. So that later you can show what was. So you can show this nightmare.*

I didn't understand why no one came to our aid. Why we were abandoned. It was unbearable: the suffering, the hunger, the death everywhere. And everybody remained silent. We were alone. There was no parachute, no camera, and I wept.

When I arrived in France, I remembered that episode. I made a point of writing a long letter to the secretary-general of the United Nations. I told him what I'd lived through and concluded by asking why nothing serious had been undertaken on behalf of Cambodia. Why I, a child and an orphan, had been so alone. Inaction was unpardonable, I said. No one could live with memories like mine.

I never received a reply from him. Nothing. Not even a simple, official note. The wounded young boy I was didn't accept that silence; the adult I am accepts it even less.

Who was the Secretary-General of the United Nations in 1979? And since 1971? Kurt Waldheim, who beginning in 1943 had been a Wehrmacht soldier under the command of the "Butcher of the Balkans," and who doubtless played a role in the bloody Kozara operation. He was surely not a war criminal, and not a Nazi, but certainly not a man of peace either. And so today I name him, because he occupied that influential post at the end of the 1970s, and because his name is a byword for dishonorable behavior and cowardice.

I FILM A KHMER ROUGE torturer who was also the commandant of the prison in his district of Steung Trang. Today he's a local notable. He's never left his district. In 1979 the Vietnamese let him stay in his post. A policeman remains a policeman. I film his hard-eyed look.

Across from him three Cham peasants talk about the cruel treatment they were subjected to. One of them describes how he was required to piss and shit in a bamboo barrel. He was no longer a man, he says. He remembers his wounds, and the bedbugs that colonized his straw mattress. Suddenly he blurts out, "Why did you torture me?"

The notable laughs. He says, "That's not the way to put the question. It's up to you to know why you're a prisoner here. If you're here, that means you're guilty!"

The peasant says, "But you know we're innocent! You know we're human!"

The notable freezes. His gestures become mechanical. He stands up and bellows, "Comrade! You are forbidden to kill the bedbugs that bite you! The guards raise them. They belong to the Angkar!" Seeing that he's frightening the peasant, he goes on: "Look how scared you are! If I hit you with a stick, you'll tell me for no reason that you're a corporal! And if I hit you again, you'll tell me you're a colonel! And if I hit you yet again, you'll tell me you're a one-star general! And if I hit you a hundred times, you're a hundred-star general! There, that's what you are!"

He and I wind up arguing. I tell him, "The Khmer Rouge era is over!" He replies, "The Khmer Rouge are everywhere, including Phnom Penh! Are you looking for trouble? Are you looking for trouble? You want to fight me?"

I say, "And why would I want to fight you? Who do you think you are, you?" I can feel that nothing has changed. Everything could start all over again, everything, so easily. Cruelty is there, right before our eyes.

One afternoon I question Duch: "This is what you say. But Huy claims just the opposite. Which of you am I to believe? And why should I believe you, you, more than him?"

Duch responds sharply, "If you believe what Huy tells you, then go talk to Huy! We should stop this whole thing. Right now. It's trite . . . You're so trite, Mr. Rithy!"

I reply, "I *am* trite. It's true. But I'm asking you questions about people who are dead. Surely that's not the best answer you can give me!"

Very calmly, Duch apologizes. He says he's tired. He stands and turns to go, followed by the guards. The session's over.

I NO LONGER WALK BAREFOOT. I write and shoot film—in other words I live a little. I'd like to escape this man, my subject, who won't stop telling me about his working methods, "You can't hesitate; you can't have a doubt in your mind; if you do, it interferes with your responsibilities as an interrogator. Even if the culprit is a member of your family, even if it's someone you trusted in the past."

Duch recounts being summoned by Son Sen and told, "Brother Nuon requires a photograph of Ly Phel's corpse." As he tells me this, Duch flies into a rage: "In my mind, I insulted Nuon Chea. The son of a bitch! We did our work in S-21 and did it well. Ly Phel had confessed. And, as was fitting, he'd been executed. But they didn't trust me! So why was I given the job in the first place?"

Therefore Duch had Ly Phel exhumed from his grave in S-21. The stench was appalling, and the men pressed their *kramas* against their faces. Duch ordered the corpse to be photographed and then reburied.

Sometimes I feel that man's hand groping for my throat, across space and time.

DUCH RECITES TO ME, in French, some lines from the poem *La mort du loup*—"The Death of the Wolf"—by Alfred de Vigny:

> *Gémir, pleurer, prier est également lâche.*
> *Fais énergiquement ta longue et lourde tâche*
> *Dans la voie où la sort a voulu t'appeler,*
> *Puis, après, comme moi, souffre et meurs sans parler.*

> (To groan, to weep, to pray are cowardly alike.
> Perform with energy your long and heavy task
> Upon the path that fate has chosen for you,
> Then afterward, like me, suffer and die in silence.)

Later I read the whole poem. A small group of hunters tracks two adult wolves and two whelps. The male wolf, surrounded and cut off from the others, seizes one of the hunters' dogs by the throat. Shot and stabbed repeatedly as he kills the dog, the wolf stoically succumbs to his wounds:

> *Il nous regarde encore, ensuite il se recouche,*
> *Tout en léchant le sang répandu sur sa bouche.*

Et, sans daigner savoir comment il a péri,
Refermant ses grands yeux, meurt sans jeter un cri.

(He looks at us once more and then lies down again,
Licking all the while the blood smeared on his mouth.
And deigning not to know how death has come to him,
He closes his great eyes and dies without a cry.)

   The hunters give up the pursuit of the other wolves. Troubled by the wolf's death, one of the men—the narrator—meditates upon what he's just witnessed:

Et ton dernier regard m'est allé jusqu'au coeur!
Il disait: "Si tu peux, fais que ton âme arrive,
À force de rester studieuse et pensive,
Jusqu'à ce haut degré de stoïque fierté
Où, naissant dans les bois, j'ai tout d'abord monté.
Gémir, pleurer, prier est également lâche.
Fais énergiquement ta longue et lourde tâche
Dans la voie où la sort a voulu t'appeler,
Puis, après, comme moi, souffre et meurs sans parler."

(And your last look went straight to my heart!
It said: "If you can, see to it that your soul,
By virtue of study and the habit of thought,
Reaches the high degree of stoic pride
To which I, forest-born, climbed from the start.
To groan, to weep, to pray are cowardly alike.

Perform with energy your long and heavy task
Upon the path that fate has chosen for you,
Then afterward, like me, suffer and die in silence.")

Duch is stoic; Duch is a wolf.

Alors il a saisi, dans sa gueule brûlante,
Du chien le plus hardi la gorge pantelante
Et n'a pas desserré ses mâchoires de fer . . .

(Then he seized in his red-hot maw
The panting throat of the bravest dog
And did not unclench his iron jaws . . .)

Duch rips the dog to pieces in his maw. He's prepared
to do anything to save the other wolves.

Jusqu'au dernier moment où le chien étranglé,
Mort longtemps avant lui, sous ses pieds a roulé.

(Until the final moment, when the throttled dog,
Dead long before him, rolled in the dirt at his feet.)

Behold Kaing Guek Eav, alias Duch, who was a good
and stoic child.

I LEFT THE DEAD ZONE. Nothingness carried on without me. After the episode of the hashish soup, I expected to be sent to some terrible work camp in the country's arid region. But instead I was assigned to a tranquil duck farm far from everything. Had the Angkar made a mistake? Did they wrongly consider that duck-raising enterprise a place of hard labor? I've never known the answers to those questions.

Two of us, a young companion and I, were placed in charge of fifty or so ducks, which like us lived in semi-freedom. A young Khmer Rouge doctor was with us, for the ducks belonged to the hospital. Regularly some local official dropped off supplies: rice for us, and bran for the ducks. In regard to everything else, we were on our own. So we'd gather leaves and roots and make soup, or we'd catch little frogs. We also did some discreet fishing. It was a strange kind of freedom, but we made the most of it.

We fed our ducks as best we could, but our days seemed empty and identical to one another. We'd never have thought of escaping; however we were often alone, sometimes for weeks. A Khmer Rouge cadre regularly passed on his bicycle to check on us. Or it was the director of the neighboring hospital, who arrived on a motorbike. Looking serious and focused, he'd make a tour of the duck farm and then question us: Was everything going all right? Did we intend to reach the targets set by the Angkar? We gave all the right answers, but we knew why he was there. After a few minutes he'd ask the young doctor to prepare a duck for him. The doctor would butcher the duck, cut it into large pieces, and turn it over to us to pluck and cook during the director's siesta.

Upon awakening, the director would devour his meal without so much as a glance our way. He'd leave the duck's feet—too lean for him—which we'd carefully save. Then, his inspection terminated, the director would bid us farewell. I remember sucking those poor ducks' feet for hours. The bird's thin skin, its hard bones, its mellow aroma of cooked poultry—what a feast!

We'd never have dared to kill a duck for ourselves. The punishment would have been terrible. When one of the little beasts got sick and died, we were required to bring its remains to the hospital and make a written report, because the duck had to be officially subtracted from the tables and our quantified targets officially adjusted. Once or twice, trembling with fear, we gobbled up a few raw eggs. But the female ducks seemed sterile and didn't do much laying.

I almost smile as I write these lines. So there were poultry farms in Democratic Kampuchea, and ducks that snorted and quacked and died of dysentery and got lost in the brushwood and sometimes met ducks stronger than they were. So some Cambodians ate duck eggs and duck meat; our farm catered primarily to the Khmer Rouge cadres. Every people has its weaknesses. I watched as hunger carried off my nephews and niece, and carried off an ideology too. The people have a belly, which eats the people—but the people don't know it.

LATER ON WE SENSED that some general upheaval had taken place. Was that around the beginning of the internal purges in 1977? I had no more notion of time. I let myself float on a dry and doleful sea. The person responsible for us disappeared from one day to the next and was replaced by an old man. I was assigned to a children's unit near the hospital, where I didn't know a soul.

There I became the steward of a group of children. I was charged with making sure they had the "necessities" (because we lived so poorly, I consider those quotation marks essential). Every morning one of the kids and I would set off to procure food at the village cooperative. Walking barefooted the two of us would transport hundreds of kilos in the course of a week: sweet potatoes, rice, and—rarely—a bit of sugar. The merchandise would be put in bags and hoisted on bamboo poles. Bamboo is incredibly supple, so with practice you could learn to walk while making the load swing in such a way that your body was propelled along and the pole didn't saw into your shoulder. I even learned to switch shoulders as I walked, without stopping. At night, we'd be exhausted. But like all the stewards, I skimmed off enough to sustain me: a handful of uncooked rice, chewed in silence on the return trip, or a sweet potato; I also remember licking a little sugar.

The atmosphere was terrible. When we woke up, some people would have disappeared. The Khmer Rouge always operated at night. Was it a guerrilla habit? Or a terror strategy? I never found out. It must be noted that very few archives or other elements from Office 870 are available today (Duch, on the other hand, left behind thousands of pages of archives in S-21, which he abandoned in a mad panic); certain messages, certain slogans are difficult to interpret. It's impossible, for example, to establish categorically whether or not Pol Pot himself wrote Democratic Kampuchea's bloody national anthem, "Glorious April 17," nor do we know for sure if, as is often claimed, he translated "The Internationale" into Khmer.

One day, when several of us were washing ourselves in a brook, I heard the leader of a children's unit say to someone else that according to the American radio, the situation on the Vietnamese front was very bad. The leader, Comrade Prem, added in an undertone, "Shit, I hope it blows up fast." Comrade Pheap, a young Khmer Rouge soldier whose morale was in decline, replied, "It would be good if it happened before the Khmer New Year! I'm sick and tired of Ta Mok's officers!" Then he turned around and realized I'd heard everything. I saw the fear in his eyes; but I was afraid too. Each of us could have denounced the others. We were all three guilty—and all convicted in advance. One (a leader, which made it worse) of having spoken in that way; another of listening to such an indiscretion without reacting and of criticizing the cadres under Ta Mok; and the third of not having denounced the first two on the spot. But would anyone have believed me? In any case a silent pact was established among us. The other two, my eighteen-year-old superiors, kept me in their unit; they wanted me where they could keep an eye on me.

Not long afterward I made an imprudent mistake. Out of weariness, perhaps. Or maybe out of pride, or the desire to provoke something. A blackboard had been installed, and one day I started writing a revolutionary slogan on it in my best Khmer calligraphy. What folly. The least sign would be interpreted and reinterpreted, and judgments were summary. The old cook saw me, came up, and snatched the chalk out of my hands. Before I could speak, he said, "Shut your trap. Erase that. If you don't, I'll do it myself." I was afraid he'd hit me, so I thought *fucking asshole* and erased the words. That man, who didn't like me, saved my life.

I ASK DUCH to define himself. He replies, in French, "I'm a stoic." The maxim came back to me all at once: endure and abstain. Stoic wisdom. Zeno's wisdom. Indifference, composure, courage.

I reply in French, "Stoic? Are you sure? To be a stoic is to forget yourself for a just cause, not to oversee the deaths of other people. You're sure you don't mean sadist?"

Duch says, "Sadist? No, I said stoic. I'm a stoic."

I continue, still in French: "How about perverse? Are you perverse?"

The torturer repeats "perverse" softly several times, but he seems hesitant about the meaning of the word. He asks me to spell it, which I do, and he writes the word on the palm of his hand. Carefully, in big letters: PERVERSE. I like to think of him returning to his cell that day, clutching an unfamiliar word in his hand. The next day I ask him if he's looked up the word in a dictionary, but he dodges the question. And his hand is clean.

Duch often laughs during our interviews. Sometimes in the midst of his laughter, he says, "You're making fun of me. You're trying to make fun of me." He laughs because he laughs. Because he's hiding his anger or his embarrassment. He also laughs to make me laugh. So we can share something. So I can understand him. He laughs so I'll be him. So I'll be a torturer in my turn, perhaps. And so I'll stop watching him.

ONE EVENING COMRADE CAU—shaved head, broad shoulders: a hard case, a "liquidator"—appeared before the group and said, "I need two kids. For a worksite. Not here, some-where else." For the past several days, we'd been hearing scuttlebutt about an imminent transfer, and we were terri-fied; rumor had it that the new location was hell itself. In the jargon we used back then, we called such a move "going to the forge." Comrade Cau's announcement was followed by a great silence.

He took a step forward and pointed to me and then to the village chief's son. I didn't understand why my com-panion would be one of the "old people," but of course I asked no questions. I picked up my spoon and my little velvet backpack, and we departed at once.

In each village, Comrade Cau was welcomed with a great deal of respect. We two boys didn't exist. We didn't have the right to speak, but we listened, and we gath-ered that we were in a difficult situation. Everyone spoke in murmurs and looked somber. Our journey lasted two days, and in the end we reached the big lake of Tonlé Sap. Our destination was another duck farm! The hell we'd been promised consisted of a few tranquil huts.

Today I believe that the village head, sensing that the adventure was turning out badly, had wanted to send his son to a safe place far from everything. But he couldn't give the impression that the boy's transfer was an indi-vidualistic choice. Hence the recent rumors that some of us would be "going to the forge." I think I was chosen because I was an orphan with no family. I'd lived in some very hard places, so I was a sort of guarantee. The chief's son didn't speak at all during the whole trip, but he seemed very calm. I think now that he knew.

In our new location there were seven of us, tending our ducks in relative autonomy . . . but we were very hungry. We fished in the lake, which was forbidden, and as a consequence of eating the fish we'd caught, we were afflicted with terrible diarrhea. Then there were some big floods, the worst we'd seen in four years. The river and the lake spread out over the land as far as the eye could see. Our hut was on the water.

One morning we saw a mountain of straw drifting toward us. I asked, "What can that be?" and so did everyone else. And then we realized that it was rice straw. We wept for joy.

We swam out to the straw and laboriously hauled the enormous mass back to the hut. All day long we beat our find with sticks, and in the end we harvested a few handfuls of rice. We were saved.

Life flowed along slowly. But then one day a man covered with mud came and called the village chief's son. The boy waved to me and left. I found out a few days later that his family had disappeared: they'd been awakened in the night, and they'd left on foot, in silence, with their hands tied behind their backs.

I'D MANAGED TO hang on to my father's wristwatch, which I kept in the very bottom of my backpack. One day the watch disappeared. I complained to Comrade Cau, who organized a general search. When he found the handsome stainless steel Omega, he nearly killed the kid who'd stolen it from me on the spot.

But was Comrade Cau perhaps less cruel than he wished to appear? He liked the watch very much and asked me if he could wear it for a period of time. I consented. Later, as we'd agreed, he gave the watch back to me.

Every Khmer Rouge cadre I ever came across displayed marks of "distinction." This notion, which I'm deliberately borrowing from Pierre Bourdieu, is more unexpected when applied to a leader in revolutionary campaigns than when it elucidates the behavior of a modern young capitalist. But are desires so easy to classify? The cadres who wore a handsome cloth beret, a watch, or real sandals were respected. They were never asked for their papers. I don't know what commanded such respect. Was it the distinctive value, whether real or imagined, of certain objects in a world without money, without anything superfluous, in a perfectly uniform world? Or was it the confiscatory power those objects attested to?

A regime's propaganda images have the merit of clearly stating its ambition. The Khmer Rouge propagandists obviously wanted to show the world smiling, enthusiastic young fighters in the bloom of health. Their productions are in every way, including visual effects, classic Communist propaganda films. But some of the images are terrible: little boys bending under the loads they're carrying, emaciated young children, and so on. You can tell that the workers in the foreground are, in fact, Khmer Rouge cadres. They're wearing real shoes; they're well-nourished, as is evident from their cheeks, their hands, their forearms; and finally, almost all of them have a pen in their shirt pocket—like Pol Pot. No small distinction. In some images taken in the jungle (no doubt before 1975), all the Angkar leaders have two or three pens in their shirt pockets—a surprising emblem for a regime proud of breaking eyeglasses and closing schools.

Comrade Cau was not at all embarrassed to display the handsome Omega. Just the opposite in fact! He let it show on purpose. Poor Panh Lauv. Had he known that one day his wristwatch would buy a bit of freedom for his son, what would he have thought?

I HAVE TROUBLE distinguishing much of a gap between the Angkar's language and the language Duch still uses in his imprisonment. In his book *Cambodia: Year Zero* (1976; first English publication 1978), François Ponchaud astutely shows how thoroughly the Angkar's language was informed by the vocabulary of war. "Struggle to catch fish"; "Struggle to produce courageously"; "Struggle to plow and rake"; "Launch an offensive for stock breeding." He gives innumerable examples: We were all "fighters," seeking "victory over flooding" and "victory over nature."

Organize. Forge. Fight. Such were the words—a steady stream of slogans—that irrigated the country, the language, our brains.

How many times did I hear the word "master"! Master of the country. Master of nature. Master of the factories. Master of everything and nothing, apparently, or so we felt, and deeply too. Who among us would have said he was the master of his days? The master of his fate? Upon arriving, however, "all the workers are as joyful as if they were just reborn."

I REMEMBER THE DAWNS when we were told, "Off to the front! Let's join the battle to cultivate the rice field!!" I myself would repeat those words in front of the Khmer Rouge cadres. Among ourselves, of course, we workers would say, "We're going to plant some rice." Had we not lived in fear, we would have found the discrepancy absurd. The Khmer Rouge leaders, then, had developed a language without dialogue, without exchange: a derivative, violent language, based on Khmer words but discarding some and inventing others. Today that peculiar mode of speech, where there was no place for emotion or doubt or confusion, has not completely disappeared.

DUCH MUTTERS LIKE a sage. He uses neutral, veiled words. Some, such as "interrogation cadre," are the fruit of ideology, and one can understand. Or "hot method" (in reference to torture), and one can guess. But he also uses words that don't necessarily stand out, words that must in fact be interpreted, for if not, who would believe the speaker to be a mass murderer? Referring to a man who was dying under torture, Duch talks about his "weakened health." Recalling the capabilities of his teams, which as we have seen he himself selected and trained, Duch insists that "My cadres knew how to strike, and all the rest." "All the rest"? On another occasion he sings the praises of what he calls "striking with forethought."

I believe that way of being and of speaking was able to fascinate people in the past and still fascinates some today. Even my friend Nath, a former prisoner in S-21, which he survived only because of Duch's good graces (Duch himself wrote on Nath's file, "Keep for use"; Nath usefully painted portraits of Pol Pot for a year and also assisted one of the sculptors)—even Nath was slow, at the time, to grasp what kind of person he was dealing with. There was, on the one hand, the educated, mild-mannered man who spoke a refined Khmer, came to see him every day, and called him "Painter Nath"; who examined his pictures, gave his assent, and smiled (not far away, electrocutions were taking place, whippings were being administered, fingernails were being torn out); and on the other hand there was the master of S-21, the head of the torture center, who never had any doubts.

Years pass; words fade away. Today Duch's language is a mixture of confession and refusal to confess. And there's the origin of his slithering, cowardly mildness, a far cry from the mathematical sequences that marked his childhood.

ONCE—ONCE IN THE course of four years—I received from the Angkar a shapeless pair of dark blue pants, which I belted with a cord as my father had done. On two occasions some Khmer Rouge doctors from the hospital gave me a black shirt. They themselves lived in fear: worse yet, in fear of fear.

I try to set out in detail the chronology of that period. How does one go back thirty-five years? And must one? No. No, I'm not going back. I'm looking. For places, dates, seasons. I organize my pages year by year. I draw arrows. I scribble. In the beginning there was Koh Thom. Then the pagoda at Koh Tauch. The hospital in Mong. The one in Battambang. Pursat province. The refugee camp in Mai Rut, across the border in Thailand. Sometimes smells come back to me. Forgotten details. I'm shivering in the rain. I make out footsteps. A buffalo brushes against me. Where are the humans? My sheet of paper and my poor black lines remain. Someone's standing behind me, crying.

THEN COMRADE CAU brought me back to the village. I attended his wedding in the presence of the Angkar. That day about fifteen couples stood before one of the district cadres to be joined in wedlock. There was no joy, no music, no dancing; instead some shouted slogans, exhorting the young couples to be faithful to the revolution and to exhibit their gratitude to the all-seeing Angkar.

Once again we took up the exhausting, placid life of the fields. One evening a man—a Khmer Rouge doctor I knew from the Mong hospital—was pulling a cart loaded with sacks of rice. In order to save time he elected to cross the rice field rather than follow the central divider strip, thus risking the possibility of getting his load stuck in the mud. He was violating the rule. Some Khmer Rouge rushed up to him. They beat him and insulted him. Then they decided to execute him. He didn't utter a cry. His body, with the back of his head smashed in, remained on the edge of the rice field for several days.

During the preparations for Duch's trial, I note these words from Mao Zedong:

I'm responsible only for the reality I know and absolutely not responsible for anything else whatsoever. I don't know the past, and I don't know the future. They have nothing to do with my own personal reality.

I'm responsible "only for the reality I know": time, history, and thought are not for humans.

IT'S THE END of winter in Paris. Sitting in a public garden I watch a child pushing a toy, a musical roller like a miniature lawn mower. His sandals are swallowed up by a tiny jungle. He hesitates, smiles, and finally falls. His young mother hurries to him and kisses him, laughing. Sometimes everything is so sweet. I apply a match to a cigar. I hold the tube of tobacco between my lips, turning it slowly. I'm elsewhere. In the tobacco, the jungle. My childhood. All at once I cry out; the match has burned my fingers. In a flash I saw the white man ringed with flaming tires, burning alive. He screamed. I shouted too. I reach down to the grass and pick up my cigar. My hand's shaking a little.

WHEN THE VIETNAMESE ARMY, together with a few units of the Cambodian resistance, took Phnom Penh on January 7, 1979, the Khmer Rouge fled in disorder. The Vietnamese were heavily armed, motorized, hardened by decades of combat.

Near Mong an armored unit made a breakthrough along the national highway. The skirmishes were brief but very violent. The Vietnamese destroyed some trains and part of the railroad station and then left for Pursat and Phnom Penh. They were probably testing the resistance of the military camp across the way before the final offensive. Or maybe they were trying to stop a Khmer Rouge train that had departed from Phnom Penh.

All our cadres disappeared at once. As though vaporized. Back to the jungle. My joy was so great that I went to fetch the white shirt I kept in the bottom of my backpack. I put the shirt on proudly. White, to celebrate life. I exclaimed, "We're free!" Whereupon, who comes running up, extremely displeased? The same old cook. He points a finger at me and barks, "Shut up! And take off that white shirt! At once!" This time I didn't just let him push me around. I said, "Come on, whenever there's good news, you try to stop us from enjoying it! The Khmer Rouge are over!" He came closer to me and said threateningly, "Take off that white shirt and hold your tongue!" There was no changing his mind. I undressed gloomily and put my black shirt back on.

A few days later the Khmer Rouge reappeared. The man who didn't like me had once again saved my life. All those who had taken advantage of the situation were slaughtered. Some of them had taken rice; others had siphoned off gasoline. They were executed with pickaxes. I waited several days before reappearing in my turn: I'd taken refuge with some midwives in my village. From then on, the Khmer Rouge cadres listened to the American radio broadcasts, and they knew the fighting was going badly for them.

I REMEMBER THAT at that time Comrade Pheap and I had determined on a very serious undertaking, namely the killing of a Khmer Rouge cadre. He was arresting dozens of men, women, and children, whom he'd tie up together, one to another. The killing machine no longer really distinguished between "old people" and "new people." The enemy was everywhere.

We were seething with anger. Prem wasn't with us, but he let us have our way. Pheap and I each took a machete. We followed that cruel man. We lay in wait for him. I imagined myself carving him up.

On the appointed day he arrived on his bike, and we sprang up, machetes in hand. But not everyone can be a murderer. The cadre slowed down and addressed us suspiciously.

"Everything all right, comrades?" He stopped.

And we lowered our eyes and said, "Everything's fine . . ."

I think about the words of Fouquier-Tinville, the public prosecutor before the Revolutionary Tribunal during the French Revolution: "Heads are falling like slates."

PHEAP AND I spent the following week dodging from one hiding place to another, from the dried-up river bed to the cornfield behind the village. We'd found a shell from an M-79 grenade launcher, and if we were denounced, we figured we'd turn the cap of the shell three times and blow ourselves up. But Comrade Prem came looking for us and placed us under his protection. Our unit then began a period of constant relocation; for two months we hardly stopped moving about. The Angkar transported the rice from the cooperative to the mountains and distributed weapons that came from no-one-knew-where to our unit and others. Prem received a Chinese CK-7. And we set out for some of the remotest areas of the country.

IN THE MOUNTAINS we received bigger rice rations; it was as though the Khmer Rouge were trying to persuade us, trying to hold on to us. The words "new people" disappeared: we were all Khmers, Cambodians, facing the Vietnamese invader. In a few hours the Angkar's rhetoric became radically nationalistic.

Tired of eating nothing but rice and salt, Pheap and I decided to go down to the Mong region and the forests near Tonlé Sap, the big lake—where we could fish.

I composed a magnificent safe-conduct document, a pass that Pheap coolly presented at each checkpoint and in each village we passed through. I remember having written, at the bottom of the document, "Long live the revolutionary, extraordinarily clear-sighted Angkar! Long live the Communist Party of Kampuchea!" No signature. Those two slogans sufficed.

With his perfectly judged official language, his black outfit, his hat, and his two pens, Pheap inspired respect. Corpses were lying here and there in deserted villages. Surrounded by chaos we continued on our way.

AS WE TRAVELED on, we came across a big man-made pond. It was practically dry, and the muddy water on its bottom was covered with scales and white eyes: hundreds of asphyxiated fish. All we had to do to gather them up was to bend down. Other men, as hungry as we were, joined us.

Two armed soldiers appeared on the embankment. One of them fired a shot in the air and then another shot closer to us. "Who gave you the right to catch those fish?" one of them asked angrily. "They belong to the collective! Who are you?" They lined us up under the white-hot sun and demanded a self-criticism. In the new context the request seemed surreal.

We sat down. Right away Pheap demanded the right to speak, rose, glared at those two lost soldiers, and addressed them in a martial tone: "Comrades! We need these fish for our comrades, encamped in the mountains. We need these fish in order to do battle against the Vietnamese enemy! Long live the Angkar! Long live the Angkar!" The rest of us, still sitting on the ground, thrust our right hands skyward and repeated, "Long live the Angkar!"

The two soldiers let us carry off the fish. And we had a fabulous meal.

WE DISPERSED. I became the person in charge of about fifteen children, all orphans seven or eight years old. We distributed all the rice that remained in the camp, each carrying a portion in his rolled-up trousers. I also carried our fishnet. Every child had his bundle. Those were all our treasures.

During the previous month in the forest, I'd suffered some terrible malaria attacks. They laid me low every other day, always after lunch, always at the same hour. When I'd start to shiver, I'd warn the children. Len, a young girl, a "new people" whom I chastely loved, would boil some water. When the shaking chills began, she'd place hot stones all over my body. Two or three of the others held me down. It was terrible. I seemed to hear my mother murmuring, "Be brave, Rithy. Be brave." The crises grew worse. I needed five or six children on top of me to stop my trembling. And after the cold came the fever. I raved; I rolled on the ground. Len applied kapok bark, which we'd gone looking for in the forest, to every part of my body. Little by little, my temperature decreased. I sank into lethargy. It's hard to last very long in the forest, but at the end of a month my fever crises became less frequent and then milder.

Discipline was breaking down on all sides. When the Vietnamese got close new slogans would appear within a few hours: "Death to Pham Van Dong!" and "Death to the Vietnamese thieves, devourers of our land!" The Khmer Rouge decided they would continue to fight and asked me to accompany them. I flatly refused. They disappeared into the scrubland along the Thai border.

The orphans went back to the village, where some families took them in and adopted them. Imagine such words, so simple, so evident: "take in"; "adopt." They meant freedom. Freedom to speak. Freedom to use words.

I met Comrade Cau again, the man I'd once considered such a tough guy. He was with his wife, and he kindly said to me, "Stay with us!" There again, I refused. I said, "I'm leaving. I have to leave. I want to be left alone. Do you understand?"

Comrade Pheap disappeared. Did he go into the jungle with the Khmer Rouge? I'll never know.

I FOUND MY BIG SISTER again. She was with her friends—incredible, isn't it? They hesitated. Not my sister and me. We set out for Thailand. Our trip, which lasted some weeks, is part of the sad history of the Cambodian refugees. The Thais beat us. Pursued us. Turned us over to the Khmer Rouge. One day we sat down and asked some Thai soldiers to execute us rather than to keep driving us back toward the jungle and the minefields.

For a time we lived near a pagoda. The Khmer Rouge were across from us, on the other side of the river. Watching us.

My sister had managed to hold on to a few gold bracelets. We buried them at the bottom of a kettleful of overcooked rice, and I carried the kettle. At night every girl slept together with two or three men, who protected her from the soldiers.

We were pushed around and scorned. Nobody wanted us. Then a journalist discovered us in the middle of the jungle and told the Red Cross about us, and that was how we came to be rescued. But two other large groups, a total of several hundred people, disappeared without a trace.

In the refugee camp in Mai Rut, Thailand, our pictures were taken. We were counted and given medical care. I can still remember the taste of tinned sardines. And the taste of my first stick of chewing gum. And the smell of trucks. How long had it been since the last time I'd smelled gasoline?

My uncle, who had returned from the United States to reconstruct Cambodia, was tortured and eliminated in S-21.

Four of my brothers were studying abroad when the Khmer Rouge entered Phnom Penh and wisely stayed where they were. Two of them were in France, one in Germany, and one in Algeria. And so, thanks to the family reunification laws, my sister and I were able to enter France.

IN JANUARY 1979, in an opinion piece entitled "Kampuchea will overcome!" and published in *Le Monde*, the philosopher Alain Badiou wrote the following:

> Apart from the tensions accumulated among the Khmer peasant class during centuries of absolute misery, the simple desire to rely on their own resources and not to be anyone's subjects clarifies a great many aspects of the Cambodian revolution, including the incorporation of terror into the revolutionary agenda. . . . No one is being requested to examine conscientiously the issue of who, in the end, is served by the formidable anti-Cambodian campaign of the past three years, or to consider whether the reality principle of that campaign is not to be found in the current attempt to arrive at a "final solution."

In 1980, in their book *After the Cataclysm*, Noam Chomsky and his coauthor, Edward S. Herman, had this to say:

> While all of the countries of Indochina have been subjected to endless denunciations in the West for

their "loathsome" qualities and unacceptable failure
to find humane solutions to their problems, Cambodia was a particular target of abuse. In fact, it became
virtually a matter of dogma in the West that the regime was the very incarnation of evil with no re-
deeming qualities, and that the handful of demonic
creatures who had somehow taken over the country were systematically massacring and starving the
population. How the "nine men at the center" were
able to achieve this feat or why they chose to pursue
the strange course of "autogenocide" were questions
that were rarely pursued.

I reread those sentences. The words slip aside and get
away. I don't understand.

IN "DUCH'S BLACK BOOK," the definition of those likely
to enter S-21 can be found. There are two cases, he explains to his young students: "those who are free and
speak freely, and those who are already under surveillance
by the Angkar." Nath the painter shows a torturer this
notebook. He asks him to read the passage and explain
it. "If you add the two cases," Nath insists, "those who
are free and speak freely plus those under surveillance by
the Angkar, who's left? Doesn't that definition encompass
all the people of Democratic Kampuchea?" The "comrade

interrogator" keeps quiet for a while, then asks that the question be repeated. He doesn't understand. He says he doesn't understand.

I DON'T KNOW whether words heal me or exhaust me. Images come; I chase after them. During the day, under the fan in my office, I unfold a cot and fall onto it. That way I don't have to fear vertigo. I'm not tempted to put an end to it.

ON CERTAIN EVENINGS a Khmer Rouge commander would drop in and point to several persons: "The Angkar has chosen you. You're to be sent away to study. We leave at once." They'd disappear together into the night, without a sound, traveling on foot. The following day they'd be found with their heads smashed. Some of the others would try to know more, to see if they could recognize a face. I never wanted to get anywhere near the victims. Never. For me, an unburied corpse is a nightmare.

The bodies stayed where they lay, dressed in their black outfits, eaten by rats and worms, glazed by the sun, submerged by the rains. They fertilized fear.

IN THE KHMER ROUGE SLOGANS, in their songs and gestures, in Duch's speech, there's an icy lyricism. The slogans are chiseled and perfectly cadenced. I think about the regime's propaganda images, about those thousands of men, women, and children armed with shovels and dancing, or so it seems, in the dust. But they're not dancing. They're parading. They're digging, carting, shoring up. They're no longer humans but elements of power. "The people" is a noria. "The people" is an idea. Is this the accomplishment of the Enlightenment—universal reason at work? Or is it the Enlightenment's end?

In those slogans, those gestures, that way of speaking, those images, I see only abstract exaltation. When the idea becomes the ideal, ask yourself the ultimate question: What about man? The answer: man? How boring . . .

Duch: "François Bizot is right. Everyone's capable of being a torturer." He points to me and laughs: "Under the Khmer Rouge, Mr. Rithy, you could have been in my place! You could have been the commandant of S-21!" He likes this idea a lot. He leans back and says, "You're so serious!" This is his method: he wants to get you on board with him, by means of laughter, by means of proximity; he wants to make you his, make you him.

I reply simply, "No."

He laughs again.

Duch is a man. And I want him to be a man. Not barricaded behind words, but returned to humanity through them.

As a child, I dreamed that a camera parachuted down to me in the night; today that camera's in my hands. Today I know why I make movies, why I write. I look at people. All people. Each in his or her place.

I REMEMBER FINDING an infant lying on the ground near the Mong road. He wasn't crying. I remember carrying him in my arms and giving him to an old woman. I can still see her, bent over the child, calling other women, looking for someone with mother's milk.

DUCH TALKS ABOUT his obsession with secrecy, which was applied absolutely in regard to S-21, to mass torture, and to Choeung Ek, the execution center, where thousands of prisoners were killed and their bodies thrown into pits. During the "seminar" he led in February 1976—a detailed account of this meeting has been conserved—Duch summarized his views in this way: "There are four secrets: I don't know, I didn't hear, I didn't see, I'm not talking."

A SPECIAL FORCES SOLDIER who was stationed in Phnom Penh relates to me how he and his men were charged with arresting people "on the list." Men and women would arrive from the provinces to "study" or to take part in a meeting with the Angkar. They were asked to place their bundles in a corner, and then came the announcement that a banquet had been prepared for them to enjoy before their meeting with a Khmer Rouge leader. After they entered the "banquet room," they were held at gunpoint and their hands cuffed behind their backs.

Then they were put in the back of a truck. No Khmer Rouge could ride with them, as they'd already been cut off from the world of humanity. The back of the truck was covered with a tarpaulin and the vehicle driven to Tuol Sleng. The truck had to stop several blocks from the entrance to S-21. Some comrades from the prison would arrive, shouting; they'd take possession of the truck, replacing its official occupants, and drive it inside; not long afterward the truck would be returned to them. S-21 was guarded and patrolled day and night. It was surrounded by fences and barbed wire that were electrified during the hours of darkness.

A further deception was practiced upon those prisoners who had confessed under torture. Did a guard, a torturer, somebody in charge, or Duch himself come and speak to the people as embodied in the condemned person? Did someone say, "Comrade, you've betrayed the regime, and you know what awaits you"? Not at all. The prisoner was blindfolded and handcuffed, and his feet, which had been chained up to that point, were freed from their fetters. The guards or the comrade torturers would say to the prisoner, "Good-bye. You're being returned to your village. Don't go back to your old ways. Try to reconstruct yourself." An incredible lie on the Angkar's part, and this while mental and physical torture was being employed with the goal of obtaining a detailed confession. . . . I suppose the lie was necessary to prevent rebellion, screams, problems, whatever would have made the transfer difficult—and broken the secrecy. But at the same time, the process of "popular" justice, the people's justice, was rendered null and void.

THE PROCEDURE IN regard to condemned prisoners was precise and strictly adhered to. In the afternoon the personnel in Choeung Ek charged with carrying out executions were informed of the exact number of prisoners they would be receiving, whereupon a grave of suitable size would be dug. After nightfall a truck brought the condemned to a spot not far from the execution grounds and near a hut. Diesel generators, operating at full force, powered bright fluorescent lights. The chained, blindfolded prisoners sat and waited in the midst of hellish noise. They were hungry, thirsty, sweating, exhausted, and often wounded. Some had been beaten for weeks. A man would be led to the edge of the pit. He knew nothing, saw nothing, heard only the general hubbub. Perhaps he thought he was about to be loaded onto another truck. He'd be pushed to his knees. Then he'd receive a violent blow to the back of his head, usually from a crowbar. He'd crumple into the big grave, where a second executioner would slit his throat. Sometimes the prisoner was dead already, but the slashed throat served in any case to drain the blood from his body, so that it wouldn't swell up and would thus decompose faster. The idea that the graves might be detected made the Khmer Rouge nervous.

Then came the next prisoner. Standing on the edge of the pit, a man oversaw the operations and verified the number of bodies on his register. There could be no discrepancy between the lists sent out from S-21 and those kept at Choeung Ek. Occasionally a prisoner would escape from the truck, and the ensuing search would cover a radius of several kilometers; eventually the prisoner would be caught. If there was the slightest discrepancy between the lists, the executioners pulled all the bodies out of the pit—dark work, bloody work—counted them, recounted them, identified them.

Then the corpses were returned to the grave and laid head-to-foot. The victims' clothes were removed and kept for reuse by other prisoners in the center. The blood-smeared handcuffs were likewise recovered, later to be rinsed off in big jars at S-21.

There was also a small detachment of guards, who kept watch over the graves along with the killers. As dawn approached, the pits were filled in and covered over. Death was a secret.

Duch claims to have visited Choeung Ek only once, on Son Sen's orders, and to have seen nothing, because "everything was done by flashlight."

When I relate this version to at least two of the torturers, they're outraged. "Duch? Only once?" "By flashlight?" Impossible, they say. They declare that they worked under fluorescent lights: "The sky was as bright as day."

The logistics of the whole operation were efficient, tried, true. It's inconceivable that Duch didn't control them from one end to the other; in his world he was the equivalent of the general secretary of the Party, and without his supervision everything in regard to the number of persons imprisoned, tortured, and murdered would have quickly turned into chaos. Duch declares, "In S-21, the Party was me," and he makes a strange, emphatic, characteristic gesture: he points to his mouth with both hands.

When I press him Duch murmurs, "I also went there with Mam Nay, but don't tell the tribunal that . . . to protect Mam Nay . . ." This sotto voce confidence epitomizes the man: he offers us a partial truth (he went to Choeung Ek more than once); a partial falsehood (he's misleading the tribunal in order "to protect Mam Nay," who's asked for nothing and who's not under prosecution); and he's fortifying a much bigger lie, since he obviously betook himself to that fateful place on many occasions. I also question him about his visits to the various detention and execution centers in the provinces—but in vain: "To Kampong Thom? That was for lunch with my brother-in-law, who was the head of the security office. To Kraing Ta Chan? No, I never went there. But there was a senior cadre there who looked a little like me and who was also called Duch."

Later on he had his brother-in-law executed at S-21.

As for me I've often made the trip from S-21 and Choeung Ek, with Huy and also with Vann Nath; at night, at the same time the convoys used to roll.

THE BANALITY OF EVIL: a seductive formula that allows all kinds of misinterpretations. I'm leery of it. It's true that Hannah Arendt's banal man—by his words, by his vision—banalizes evil. So I understand the formula as "the banalization of evil," as if there were nothing but functionaries, nothing but cogs in the extermination machine. As if there were only men working in offices. As if there were nobody in charge and no deliberate plan. A world of gearwheels and racks and pinions and bloodstained axes.

Stanley Milgram's study, known as the Milgram Experiment, tends in the same direction: In the laboratory every individual is capable of giving a stranger a painful or fatal electric shock. Every individual can become an executioner. He need only submit, obey, perhaps even enjoy obeying. But what about the person who doesn't submit?

I don't deny that some executioners and torturers can be ordinary people or that an ordinary person may become an executioner and torturer. But I believe in the uniqueness of the individual. I'm interested in his past, in his emotional, familial, intellectual trajectory, and in the society in which he developed. And so Duch conceived torture methods, refined them, taught them. He annotated files. Recruited torturers. Trained his teams. Spurred them on. Duch reported to his superiors. Participated in discussions with them. He was continually in control of his actions, continually aware of them.

Duch wasn't the director of a prison; he was the commandant of S-21, the center that reported directly to Office 870, the center nobody got out of alive, the center where even very high-ranking leaders of the regime could be "processed."

I return to my formula: neither sacralization nor banalization. Duch isn't a monster or a fascinating torturer. Duch isn't an ordinary criminal. He's a *thinking man*. He's one of the people responsible for the extermination. One must consider his career path: if he could refine his methods in M-13, it was no longer necessary to do so in S-21; if he could spare a man in M-13, he spared no one in S-21. This man of blood, who sees himself as a bureaucrat, tells me confidentially, "Words were my spears."

LET ME RETURN to the account given by the Special Forces soldier mentioned earlier and summarize his words again: his unit arrested people whose names were on a list; once arrested the prisoners were immediately placed in the back of a truck, to be conveyed to the torture center; no Khmer Rouge could travel in the back with them; the truck was covered with a tarp and driven to the center; when the truck reached a point not far from the center, the driver had to stop; comrades from S-21 came and took possession of the truck and drove it inside the prison.

The enemies lists were drawn up by the Angkar: this process involved investigation, verification, and arrest, the real "police work," even though the police in question were obviously political police, violent and blindly obedient. Duch, for his part, took delivery of the prisoners and organized their mental and physical torture. He was in charge of the state's and the party's "internal security forces," for which the Khmer Rouge invented the composite word Santebal. Could Duch obtain and verify confessions, when he never left his post in the prison? Could he carry out cross-checks, when he never confronted his prisoners? Could he analyze the lists of persons who had been denounced to the authorities? No. And what to think about confessions extracted after weeks of torture? We also know that the torturers required prisoners to admit that they were in the pay of the KGB or the CIA or the Vietnamese. How simple proletarian truth was!

In such a system, the prisoner knows nothing; the torturer knows nothing. It wasn't a matter of exploring reality; the business at hand involved the construction of a story, followed by extermination. To situate his activity within the human world, the world of normal politics, Duch uses the word "police"; but it's a lie.

Duch: "And to think, I wanted to bring knowledge to the people. I've fallen very low."

THESE DAYS ONE of the S-21 executioners tends his vegetable garden, his mind totally serene. He's become his village's mediator. People consult him about family quarrels or problems with neighbors. But how can a lasting peace be established when genuine justice doesn't exist? How must we envision the fate of his country?

TODAY I'M WALKING around Phnom Penh. There aren't any sidewalks, just arrangements of asphalt and dusty paving stones. Once you're used to it, you don't trip anymore. The air is broiling, and the noise never stops: passing trucks, skidding motorbikes, sounding horns. I see the cheerful faces of the passersby, boys in jeans, girls in bright skirts, their flip-flops slapping the street. My neck is sweaty, like my hands and my shirt. I smoke and think about my family. I think about those four years, which aren't a nightmare, which are neither dream nor nightmare, even though I still have plenty of nightmares. Let's call it a complicated chapter in my life. And one which

I'll never forgive. For me, forgiveness is something very private.

Only politicians arrogate to themselves the right to grant reprieves or pardons in the name of all—a right unimaginable when mass crimes or genocides are concerned. I don't believe in reconciliation by decree. And whatever's too quickly resolved scares me. It's peace of soul that brings about reconciliation and not the reverse.

I place more credence in pedagogy than in justice. I believe in working over time, in the working of time. I want to understand, explain, and remember—in precisely that order.

A MOTHER LEARNS that all her children have been executed by the Angkar. She doesn't know what they were accused of. She doesn't know how they died. She doesn't know where their bodies are. They're children of *kamtech*. So she gathers stones and stuffs them into the sleeves of her shirt and the cuffs of her black trousers. She makes herself necklaces and bracelets of stones. When she feels she's ready, she walks heavily to the riverbank and down into the thick water. Her ankles disappear. Her thighs. Soon afterward, her waist. Then her stomach goes under, and her shoulders. In their turn, her neck, her chin, her cheeks, her mouth vanish. Her forehead. The drowned woman keeps on walking to the bottom of the river. A peasant told me this story.

MY FILMS ARE oriented toward knowledge; everything is based on reading, reflection, research work. But I also believe in form, in colors, in light, in framing and editing. I believe in poetry. Is that a shocking thought? No. The Khmer Rouge didn't break everything. And we must learn all over again. Silence wounds. Silence about the blood-takings, the vivisections, the murdered children. Silence about the rapes: when one lives in cruelty, even sexual relations are cruel.

Today I'd like a book full of gentle words. As I traverse the countryside around Battambang, the rich province where I was once so hungry and so afraid, I gaze at its landscape of impassive rice fields. At the poor villages beside the road. At the water vendors shuffling along in worn-out shoes. At the spiky jungle, rising up against the blue sky. Now there are parabolic antennas and teenagers talking on telephones. Where's the past? Where's my childhood? Tears come to my eyes. I clench my fists.

IF SOME PEOPLE can maintain that the Nazi gas chambers were a "detail" in the history of the Second World War, then every mass crime in history is liable to be considered, one day or another, in France or elsewhere, a "detail." The crime in Cambodia, for example. I have therefore striven to go into the tiniest details; to verify once, twice, a hundred times; never to give up on the chance of meeting a torturer or a survivor; to verify the organization of S-21. I want the truth to be established and documented. If every detail of the story I recount is incontestable, then the mass crime committed in Cambodia will never be a "detail."

I find it unacceptable that the tribunal's prosecutors show a photograph of a swollen corpse lying on an iron bed and offer no real explanation.

I find it unacceptable that the prosecutors in the tribunal's courtroom show a "fictional documentary"—I can give it no other name—where actors in topnotch physical shape play prisoners with shackled feet, lying on the ground in S-21. . . . Is there really any lack of evidence? No. Dozens of photographs taken by "comrades" in S-21 exist. There are even photographs of a prisoner who committed suicide and of another with a bullet wound in his head, shot because he tried to resist. The man in the photo is going to die; Duch immediately says his name and then describes the "accident." What an admission!

A document of that sort must be analyzed, dissected, considered in its context. In itself it's not a proof. The story it contains is a proof, but that story isn't given. It is to be sought. In his memoir *The Politics of Memory*, Raul Hilberg writes that a document is

> first of all an artifact, immediately recognizable as
> a relic. It is the original paper that was once upon a

time handled by a bureaucrat and signed or initialed
by him. More than that, the words on that paper
constituted an *action*: the performance of a function.
If the paper was an order, it signified the *entire* action
of its originator.

I find it unacceptable that a prosecutor doesn't make
thorough use of S-21's trove of extremely well-kept records,
written in inks of three different colors, which Duch proudly
describes before my camera. Such documents signify. They
speak. Those records should have been presented to the accused and explanations demanded. I find it incomprehensible that the tribunal didn't call Nuon Chea as a witness.

And lastly I find the allegedly "neutral" images shot by
the ECCC's technicians unacceptable. In this realm there
is no neutrality. The result was a trial without images for
a genocide without images. To film a trial such as this
would have been to advance the cause of knowledge; it
would have conduced to reflection upon the regime's politics and the men who implemented them; it would have
offered a look at history. But this work was left undone.

On the other hand the presence of the plaintiffs was
important, and so was the decision to hold the trial in
Phnom Penh and not elsewhere. Because of this, Cambodians took an interest in the trial and followed it on the
television news or in the newspapers.

In his "Black Book," Duch spells it out clearly: the victim himself must believe his confession. He invents an

almost true confession. If the confession is false, what legitimacy can interrogation have? And in Duch's case what legitimacy was there to living in the name of the Angkar? It was a hideous sophism. The man lived in a world where the confession he received became the truth—at the price of what torments?—and thus it is that he can stand his ground without falling to pieces today.

If a prisoner wrote in one of his confessions that he'd lied in a previous one, if he took back the names he'd given or denied the existence of the traitorous rings he'd identified, if he swore that this time he'd tell the truth, the torture would resume. And continue until the prisoner himself no longer contested his own version. The procedure constituted the truth—even if the talking mouth belonged to a piece of refuse.

A MYSTERY REMAINS: When would Duch decide that he'd reached the "truth"? Why did he choose one version over another?

IF YOU EXAMINE certain confessions in detail and follow them through successive versions, you can see small signs of resistance begin to appear: some surprising sentences, for example, or recurring formulas. You can also see moments of sincerity, though I have trouble applying that word to those prisoners, many of whom had been undergoing torture for weeks. Consider a statement that ends like this:

> I know I'm going to die. I can't hold on anymore. I accept death. I remain a son of the Angkar. Long live the Communist Party of Democratic Kampuchea!

The Khmer Rouge atrociously slaughtered people who were Chams, Chinese, Vietnamese, Khmer Krom; but in the great majority of cases, the person they killed was another of themselves. That was also the reason why the confession had to be supported. Even the executioner had to be convinced that he was carrying out a legitimate death sentence, and that the condemned was an enemy of the people. I remember Duch's remark: "Comrades under arrest were enemies, not men."

SEVERAL WITNESSES ATTEST that some prisoners, alerted by the sight of the guards and the barbed wire, entered S-21 well aware of what was awaiting them, stood in the courtyard, raised their fists, and cried out, "Long live the Communist Party of Democratic Kampuchea!"

I'VE RECENTLY LEARNED that some families of ethnic minorities in the northern part of the country, realizing that the arrival of the Khmer Rouge meant the end of them, decided to flee into the rainforest. They took up residence there, in the midst of impenetrable jungle, where even the revolutionaries wouldn't dare to go. Those peasants lived in hiding, forgotten by all. They learned to survive in destitution. Despite the wild animals, the snakes, the spiders, despite the climate and the humidity. They grew whatever food they could grow. They hunted. They ate tree bark, roots, fish. They tended their sick and injured. They married. They had children. Of course they lived without electricity, without potable water, without medicine, without paper, without books. Without us—if I dare put it like that. When their old clothes wore out, they made themselves new outfits of leaves and lianas.

In 2009 one of those survivors ventured out of the jungle and approached a village. He was astounded to discover that the Khmer Rouge had left. Soon the whole group abandoned their encampment and returned to civilization.

According to the latest reports, the jungle folk have built houses for themselves in the village and are trying to get used to our world. It's not easy for them. Along with adapting to the strangeness, beauty, and madness of modern life, they must also relearn the laws, the concept of private property, the use of money. They've lived in a harsh but egalitarian world—a state of Rousseauian perfection.

These days, they get sick a lot, they who survived thirty years in the jungle.

⸺

DUCH: "The course the Party would take was set in a document entitled *The Political Course as an Essential Component of the Revolutionary Strategy in Cambodia*. It was made official on September 30, 1960."

DUCH: "I wasn't an outlaw because there wasn't any law. I followed the Party's course. After the victory of April 17, we put the entirety of that course into practice. We'd won the war, and we were going to be done with the bourgeois and capitalist classes and done with their regimes. The people were sent to the rice fields. Not only the bourgeois, the capitalists, and other senior officials, but also students, professors, doctors, engineers. . . . All were sent to the provinces to do productive work. The goal of our revolution was to present Cambodia with only two classes: workers and peasants. I myself taught that ideology during the day of study held on June 24, 1975."

ME: "But why starve people? Why not look after them? Why eliminate them? Why kill children? Did they not fit into either of those classes? Two months after your victory, you were preparing people to kill not imperialists but 'the enemy.' Who was the enemy?"

Duch rubs his face, fixes his eyes on me, and smiles. How can I hope his attitude will change? He considers himself a revolutionary and wishes to enter history with that title. That's the way his logic works. From here on, he wants to write his history, their history—and this trial provides him with a platform.

Before the trial court and then before the appeals court, Duch publicly requests "that he be set free." The judge questions Duch's lawyer: "What is your client asking for?" The lawyer confirms Duch's request: "For release." Why is this man—who never released anyone from S-21, the prison he directed so assiduously—asking for release? "I applied myself. I never violated discipline," he repeats over and over again. "My wife complained. I was always poring over my files. I didn't hear my child crying." He was a very busy man. Passionate about his work.

DUCH HAS MADE an about-face. He's broken our pact of sincerity. After the pleadings, he's refused to see me. Maybe he doesn't want to talk about his request for release—which was incomprehensible, given what he's admitted to in front of my camera. Maybe he didn't want me to start questioning him again. However, he declared to the tribunal that "his door remains open to any victim who wishes to meet with him" and that "he wishes to tell the truth to all those who want to hear it."

I keep that statement in my memory, but he's made so many others, such as, "Certain things went beyond what was acceptable, and yet I did them." And so I've used photographs. Record books. Witness statements. The famous "Black Book." I've presented evidence. Compared images. Duch has a weakness: he doesn't know cinema. He doesn't believe in the play of repetitions, of intersections, of echoes. He doesn't know that montage is a politics and a morality unto itself. And in time there's only one truth.

HE SAYS TO ME, "Ah, your father, I knew him!" This is one more lie: how could he have known my father personally? I reply, "Stop, Mr. Duch. Lots of professors and teachers knew my father's name."

THE EXECUTIONER NEVER falls silent. He talks. Talks endlessly. Adds. Erases. Subtracts. Recasts. And thus he builds a history, already a legend, another reality. He hides behind speech.

I'VE NEVER HATED the man. Sometimes, when his lies surpass the limit, he even makes me laugh. I'll say, "You

know, Mr. Duch, I too was living in Democratic Kampuchea at that time." One morning he asks me, "Did
you study psychology in school?" I gather that some of
my questions must have been pretty close to those posed
by the psychiatrists—a Frenchwoman and a Cambodian
man—who are preparing their evaluations for the tribunal, particularly questions about his dreams. So I bring
them up again, and he says, "I have dreams sometimes; it's
true. I see Son Sen. He's coming toward me. He talks to
me. He gives me orders. And I obey them. It's always that
way; I obey him, never the reverse!"

"But he was your boss!" I point out. "That's the way he
probably acted in reality. . . . And in any case you were his
subordinate!" Duch never stops describing the hierarchy,
his place in it, and his "comrade interrogators"; it's part of
his well-known defense: he was only a cog, a link between
the political deciders and the people who did the dirty
work. A man of file folders. A terrible dreamer who obeys
even in his dreams.

ONE DAY, DUCH SAYS, he got a telephone call from Son Sen
on the secure line. As the call went on Duch found he had
to go to the bathroom, but he didn't dare interrupt his boss.
I press him: "But why didn't you tell him?" The response:
"I didn't dare." Son Sen kept talking. When Duch couldn't
contain himself any longer, he pissed on the tiled floor of his

office, all the while holding up his end of the conversation. I ask him, "Is that true? You pissed on the floor?" Duch: "As a child I was taught to be tidy." He laughs and then explains, "I cleaned up the mess myself."

Duch was afraid of his boss. Duch pissed on the floor like a child. Duch laughs when he tells this story. Duch is human.

If he's terrorized today by the things he did, I can understand that. If he's terrorized because he didn't save anyone, I can understand that too. He intentionally merges the terror he feels today with his former ruthlessness (which he still calls, in the language of the Angkar, his "firm stance"). But his failure to acknowledge *in detail* what for a period of years he did or caused to be done prevents him from advancing along the way to the human community. He remains far from us. Nonetheless I have this wishful notion that he'll come closer, as if conversing with me could give him a little of the humanity he's lacking. I'm very naïve. A part of me has remained behind, and it's still in those years.

For weeks I was on the alert, watching for a look. For a word. I would have abandoned my film project in exchange for a few phrases. But Duch does not advance.

WHEN YOUR DRINKING WATER comes from the rice fields, you need to be uncommonly strong to stage any sort of revolt. Unfortunately another interpretation is wide-spread: the crime against humanity committed in Cambodia was *specific* to it, partly explicable by a certain quietism connected with Buddhism, and also by a tradition of peasant violence. As if the genocide was cultural, even foreseeable.

That analysis seems facile to me. Moreover I think it implies a license to disregard intellectual mistakes, moral mistakes, strategic mistakes. Such an approach makes it easier to pass over the French protectorate; the American commitment to Lon Nol's regime, and the implacable bombing; the weakness of the successive governments; Marxist ideology; Chinese backing. It's a long list! Apparently taking an interest in the variants of Buddhism is preferable to considering the universality of the mass crime in Cambodia. But like it or not the history of Cambodia is in the deepest sense our history, human history.

I was amazed to hear a historian, speaking on a French radio station, explain that the Cambodians have been fighting among themselves since the building of Angkor. I wrote to the program's producer to let him know that what the historian had said was unacceptable—and a bit skimpy, given the fact of 1.7 million dead. I let him know that the Khmers were not some man-eating tribe. He's never replied. The fact that two clips from my film *S21* were played during the same broadcast made it all the more regrettable. I've always explicitly refused to allow my film to be cut up into segments without my consent, but my pedagogical wishes haven't been respected. And that's where we are: confusion. Or silence. Silence about Cambodia.

As for me I believe in the universality of the Khmer Rouge's crime, just as the Khmer Rouge believed in the universality of their utopia. To quote Duch: "We were destroying the old world in order to build a new one. We wanted to manufacture a new conception of the world."

IN RECENT YEARS Paris has become something of a refuge for me, a kind of womb. It's where I'm at the right distance. At the same time it's the place where I have the most absurd, most violent dreams.

Phnom Penh is different. It's the city of my childhood, the city I was run out of. I've never been able to return to my parents' house, which is occupied by other people today. When I went back to Cambodia at the beginning of the 1990s, I had a lot of trouble getting myself accepted. Since my papers had been destroyed by the Khmer Rouge, I traveled with a French passport; as a result, in Cambodia, I was considered a "Foreign Cambodian" and put under surveillance. It was even said that I was Chinese or Korean. Still today, some people look at me oddly, even those I've known since before the terrible years began. Only the youngsters who work with me call me, affectionately, "Uncle Rithy."

SOME YEARS AGO I proposed that some university theses be produced simultaneously in French and in Khmer by French and Cambodian historians. My idea was simple: to work on a double point of view, which would be both historically fascinating and necessary; to establish, little by little, a real school of Cambodian history.

There are countless possible subjects: famine and food independence; Pol Pot's speeches; the Angkar's language and its sources; the Khmer Rouge leaders' sojourns in France; the process of dehumanization; M-13. And also the treatment of the Khmer Rouge revolution in the French press, particularly during the years 1975 and 1976, as well as the ways certain intellectuals evoked or analyzed that "experiment." Or, more simply: nourishment under the Khmer Rouge; clothes; revolutionary medicines; the mystery of the Angkar's archives. There's still a great deal to discover. A great deal.

IN S-21, EVERY AFTERNOON, Duch took a break. From anxiety? From the frenzy of beatings? From the body count? Or was it just from overwork? He'd pour a little coconut milk in a glass of Cointreau. I envision him in his office, sitting behind a stack of folders; or leaning against the wall with half-closed eyes; or standing by a window; or on a

terrace. All day, since early in the morning, the screaming hasn't stopped. A few buildings away, a man is being
electrocuted.

I PUT SOME large photographic prints on the table in front
of Duch. He understands right away: he's looking at faces
from S-21, pictures taken when the prisoners arrived at
the center, before the blows, before the torture. Women,
children, men: all afraid. They may not know what's in
store for them, but they're sad and serious. They're already
elsewhere. Duch asks me why I'm always showing him
photographs.

"What's the point?" he asks, in that tone of his.

I answer, "But the thing is . . . they're listening to you.
Koy Thourn is here. Bophana's here. Taing Siv Leang too.
I believe they're listening to you." Such simplicity is neces-
sary when faced with the immensity of the crime.

Visibly uncomfortable, Duch asks me, "May I bring a
Bible next time? I know we don't agree, but I'd like to
have it near me."

I answer, "The Bible won't save you. You ought to leave
it alone."

The next day, he puts the book on the table, a little to
his right: a weapon against the faces.

THE WELL-KNOWN PHOTOGRAPHS from S-21, taken by photographers of the regime stationed in the prison for years and perforce aware of the crime being committed there, have been shown abroad. Without any real explanation. Producing an effect like that of a work of art, an organized work of representation: all those somber faces, side by side, are humanity itself. They're among us. They watch us. That's certainly the case today in S-21, which has become a place of memory and meditation; but not in a big foreign museum, if the subjects' status and history are not explained. The ugliness of beauty.

Ang Saroeun, a Khmer Rouge photographer, was sent "to the front" to photograph dike–construction projects. He pointed his camera at some starving people and focused on them. As a result, he was arrested and sent to S-21, where he underwent torture and was subsequently executed.

I question Nhiem Ein, one of the S-21 photographers, who saw thousands of prisoners destined for torture and death pass before his lens: "What makes a photograph good?"

He replies, "The pupils of the eyes have to be in sharp focus."

I hesitate and then ask, "But why?"

He stares at me: "So they can be recognized if they escape."

DUCH SUMMONED SRIENG, another of the center's photographers, and asked him to photograph the moon for him; then an execution; and then his wife and children.

During a period spent in the provinces, Srieng likewise photographed the famine. He showed images of starving children to Duch, who said nothing. Terrified, Srieng destroyed his film and his prints.

DUCH TALKS ABOUT his companions in the tribunal's prison. They talk to one another. Take their walks together. Ieng Sary had a tray of fruit delivered to Nuon Chea. Duch even goes into details: "Nuon Chea loves to tell jokes."

DUCH'S FRENCH LAWYER has given him Stéphane Hessel's anthology of his "necessary poems," *O ma mémoire—La poésie, ma necessité,* containing poems in French, English, and German. In his introduction Hessel, who survived the Buchenwald and Dora concentration camps and barely escaped hanging, explains how the poems in the anthology helped him to endure.

I film Duch reading this collection, but I'm uneasy. Seeing that lovely book in such hands gives me pause. Am I recording the transformation of the executioner into a victim? An advance on the road to humanity? Or a scene carefully set up by Duch?

He explains his conversion to Christianity. It was the Church that made the Berlin Wall come down, he informs me with conviction. Pope John Paul II defeated Communism. And then he says, "Communism betrayed me, and so it was completely natural that I would turn to Christianity."

He was baptized in a river, but under a false name.

Duch reads the Bible every day. He appears to meditate. He regularly receives visits from evangelical pastors. If Jesus on the cross pardoned the bad thief, who was himself on a cross, what will He not do for Duch, who admits everything and wants to take everything on his own shoulders? Joining the spiritual lineage of the guilty but glorious, but saved, Duch murmurs, with his eyes turned heavenward, "I offer up my broken heart, my torment." And also, "I assume the entire responsibility for S-21." I recall that he told me one day, "My subordinates were my flesh and my blood," as if all his statements from then on were going to be larded with redemption. As if taking on the suffering one has caused, along with that of the world in general, were enough to gain a place on the side of the saved. At the right hand of the Father, not among criminals.

ME: "Why didn't God open your eyes when you were carrying out your horrible task?"

DUCH: "Leave God out of this. And don't mock religion."

I BELIEVE I'VE FAILED to mention that Democratic Kampuchea kept its seat at the United Nations until 1991, and that Pol Pot died in the jungle in 1998. In the jungle, and in his bed. And it seems so hard to try five of the regime's top leaders, currently incarcerated in Phnom Penh, with any sort of vigor. France has yet to establish what happened inside the very walls of its embassy in April 1975 or to explain why it handed over to the Khmer Rouge various leading Cambodian officials clearly destined to be put to death. As for the United States and China, will they ever reveal the ties they maintained with that criminal regime for so long, and why?

> In May 1980 the CIA produced a "demographic report" on Cambodia which denied that there had been *any* executions in the last two years of the Pol Pot regime. (The toll from executions in 1977–78 had in fact been around half a million people.)

I find these terrible lines, translated into French, in a book entitled *Le génocide au Cambodge, 1975–1979: Race, idéologie, et pouvoir*. The author, Ben Kiernan, an Australian professor at Yale University, is the founder of the remarkable Cambodian Genocide Program at the Yale Center for International and Area Studies.

I READ CHARLOTTE DELBO'S ACCOUNTS, magnificent in their simplicity, of life and survival in the Nazi concentration camps. Here are the last lines of "The Measure of Our Days," the final volume of her trilogy, *Auschwitz and After*:

> *A man ready to die for another*
> *that's something to look for*
> *don't say this any longer Beggar*
> *don't say this anymore*

I would have liked to know her. To film her. I would have liked to make a portrait of her. I believe her presence would have encouraged me. I know she carried her camp number—31661—tattooed on her forearm. I know she survived Auschwitz as well as Ravensbrück. But I came too late: she died in 1985.

ONE DAY DUCH quietly remarks, "God says that courts and tribunals are the things of men. My flesh and my blood—men can do with them what they will. As for my soul, God has already recognized my soul." Duch's eyes are raised to heaven. I see the young man he was, at the Lycée Sisowath and in the jungle. While my camera's rolling, his voice is soft. The killer's never far away.

JACQUES LACAN: "The world is hell for the man who doesn't believe in the devil." Duch is neither devil nor god. But the fact that he's man, entirely man, subtracts nothing from his uniqueness. On the contrary. He's a man who can't be anyone else, and nobody else can be him.

AFTER THE DEPARTURE of the Khmer Rouge from Phnom Penh, our big family house there was photographed. Someone recently showed me that empty, enigmatic image. The tall, unfinished dwelling in the photo is my childhood. Down in the yard, we kept chickens so that we could have lots of eggs. We had ducks too. My brother was in charge of the farmyard, and my mother tended the kitchen garden behind the house. We had mint, chili peppers, mango trees, tomatoes, lemon grass. My mother would prepare brine, in which she'd soak fish before removing and drying it.

I remember that we spent long afternoons in the kitchen with her, getting ready for the Festival of the Dead. Pans would be stacked up on the shelves. A big soup pot would be simmering away. There would also be sliced pork, caramel egg pudding, boiled chickens hanging from a bamboo stalk, rice cakes with banana filling. Our country cousins would bring cinnamon apples and jackfruit. There was so much that we didn't know what to do with it. We'd make use of our wooden food safe. We'd laugh.

I'M COMING TO THE END of this book. I've told many stories. I've seen the faces of my loved ones. I've shown a man with a unique destiny. The tribunal gave him a relatively mild sentence. Had he been a revolutionary and a courageous man, he would have told the truth. It's not up to the justice system to do that—justice isn't the truth—but to Duch alone. To tell the truth and then to die: steps on the road to mankind.

Duch is in his place. No one else can take it.

I'VE EVOKED THE WORLD of yesterday so that the bad part of it may not come back again. Let it live in our memories and in books, in the flesh of the survivors, in the monuments to the lost; and let it remain there. I undertook this project with the idea that man is not fundamentally wicked. Evil's nothing new; nor is good, but as I've written, there's also a banality of good; and an everydayness of good.

As for the good part of that former world—my childhood, my sisters' laughter, my father's silences, the tireless play of my little nephew and niece, my mother's courage and kindness, this country of stone faces, the ideas of justice, of liberty, of equality, the taste for knowledge, education—that part can't be erased. It's not a bygone day, it's an effort and a work in progress; it's the human world.

BIBLIOGRAPHY

Althusser, Louis. *For Marx.* Translated by Ben Brewster. London: Verso, 1969.

Antelme, Robert. *The Human Race.* Translated by Jeffrey Haight and Annie Mahler. Marlboro, Vermont: The Marlboro Press, 1992.

Arendt, Hannah. *Eichmann in Jerusalem: A Report on the Banality of Evil.* New York: Viking, 1963.

———. *The Origins of Totalitarianism.* New York: Schocken, 1951.

Balibar, Étienne. *La crainte des masses: politique et philosophie avant et après Marx.* Paris: Éditions Galilée, 1997.

Chandler, David. *A History of Cambodia.* 4th ed. Boulder, Colorado: Westview Press, 2007.

———. *Voices from S-21: Terror and History in Pol Pot's Secret Prison.* Berkeley, University of California Press, 2000.

Chomsky, Noam, and Edward S. Herman. *After the Cataclysm: Postwar Indochina & the Reconstruction of Imperial Ideology.* Vol. 2 of *The Political Economy of Human Rights.* London: Spokesman Books, 1980.

Delage, Christian. *La Vérité par l'image: De Nuremberg au procès Milosevic.* Paris: Éditions Denoël, 2006.

Delbo, Charlotte. *Auschwitz and After.* Translated by Rosette C. Lamont. New Haven: Yale University Press, 1995.

Deron, Francis. *Le process des Khmers rouges: Trente ans d'enquête sur le génocide Cambodgien.* Paris: Gallimard, 2009.

Figes, Orlando. *The Whisperers: Private Life in Stalin's Russia*. New York: Henry Holt, 2007.

Furet, François. *Interpreting the French Revolution*. Translated by Elborg Forster. Cambridge, England: Maison des Sciences de l'Homme and Cambridge University Press, 1981.

Hatzfeld, Jean. *Life Laid Bare: The Survivors in Rwanda Speak*. Translated by Linda Coverdale. New York: Other Press, 2007.

———. *Machete Season: The Killers in Rwanda Speak*. Translated by Linda Coverdale. New York: Farrar, Straus and Giroux, 2005.

Hessel, Stéphane. *O ma mémoire – La poésie, ma nécessité*. Paris: Seuil, 2006.

Hilberg, Raul. *The Destruction of the European Jews*. New Haven: Yale University Press, 2003. First published in 1961.

———. *The Politics of Memory: The Journey of a Holocaust Historian*. Chicago: Ivan R. Dee, 1996.

Kane, Solomon. *Le dictionnaire des Khmers rouges*. Montreuil: Aux lieux d'être, 2007.

Kiernan, Ben. *Le genocide au Cambodge, 1975–1979: Race, idéologie, et pouvoir*. Paris: Gallimard, 1998.

Klemperer, Victor. *The Language of the Third Reich: A Philologist's Notebook*. Translated by Martin Brady. London: Continuum, 2002.

Lanzmann, Claude. *The Patagonian Hare: A Memoir*. Translated by Frank Wynne. New York: Farrar, Straus and Giroux, 2012.

Levi, Primo. *The Periodic Table*. Translated by Raymond Rosenthal. New York: Schocken Books, 1984.

———. *The Reawakening* (original English title: *The Truce*). Translated by Stuart Woolf. London: The Bodley Head, 1965.

———. *Survival in Auschwitz* (original English title: *If This Is a Man*). Translated by Stuart Woolf. London: The Orion Press, 1959.

Locard, Henri. *Pol Pot's Little Red Book: The Sayings of Angkar*. Chiang Mai, Thailand: Silkworm Books, 2004.

Milgram, Stanley. *Obedience to Authority: An Experimental View*. New York: Harper & Row, 1975.

Ponchaud, François. *Cambodia: Year Zero*. Translated by Nancy Amphoux. New York: Henry Holt, 1977.

Prévert, Jacques. *Paroles*. Paris: Gallimard, 2004.

Sereny, Gitta. *Into that Darkness*. New York: McGraw-Hill, 1974.

Short, Philip. *Pol Pot: Anatomy of a Nightmare*. New York: Henry Holt, 2004.

Tackett, Timothy. *When the King Took Flight*. Cambridge: Harvard University Press, 2004.

Todorov, Tzvetan. *Facing the Extreme: Moral Life in the Concentration Camps*. Translated by Arthur Denner and Abigail Pollak. New York: Henry Holt, 1996.

Vann Nath. *A Cambodian Prison Portrait: One Year in the Khmer Rouge's S-21*. Translated by Moeun Chhan Nariddh. Bangkok: White Lotus, 1998.

Welzer, Harald. *Täter: Wie aus ganz normalen Menschen Massenmörder werden*. Frankfurt: Fischer, 2005.

Wiesel, Elie. *Night*. Translated by Marion Wiesel. New York: Hill and Wang, 2006 (revised edition).

RITHY PANH is an internationally and critically acclaimed documentary film director and screenwriter. His films include *S21: The Khmer Rouge Killing Machine* and *Rice People*, the first Cambodian film to be submitted for an Oscar. His two most recent documentaries were inspired by *The Elimination—Duch, Master of the Forges of Hell* and *The Missing Picture*, which won the Prix Un Certain Regard at the 2013 Cannes International Film Festival. Panh is the first Cambodian to win the award. The same year, he was named Asian Filmmaker of the Year at the Busan International Film Festival. His recent documentaries include *Graves Without a Name*, which was submitted as the Cambodian entry for the 2018 Oscars, and *Irradiated*, which competed for the Golden Bear at the 2020 Berlin International Film Festival.

CHRISTOPHE BATAILLE is a French novelist. His works include the award-winning *Annam*, *Hourmaster*, and *Absinthe*. He has been an editor at Editions Grasset since 1997.

JOHN CULLEN (1942–2021) was the translator of many books from Spanish, French, German, and Italian, including Yasmina Khadra's Middle East Trilogy (*The Swallows of Kabul*, *The Attack*, and *The Sirens of Baghdad*), Kamel Daoud's *The Meursault Investigation*, Manuel de Lope's *The Wrong Blood*, and Philippe Claudel's *Brodeck*.

LUKE LEAFGREN is an assistant dean of Harvard College. In addition to translating from French, he has translated seven novels from Arabic. His most recent translation is Nasser Abu Srour's prison memoir, *The Tale of a Wall* (Other Press, 2024).